Belgique – België – Belgium – Belgien

D. Fromont

Belgique
België
Belgium
Belgien

Meddens

© Les Ateliers d'Art graphique Meddens, s.a., 141-143 avenue de Scheut — 1070 Bruxelles (Belgique)

Dépôt légal : D/1972/0062/36 - 085/3ᵉ trimestre 1972

2ᵉ édition 1973

Printed in Belgium

Les Belges
et leur petite patrie
aux rives de la Mer du Nord

Het Belgische volk
en het land
aan de oevers van de Noordzee

Comme tous les peuples d'Europe, le peuple belge est d'une composition ethnique extrêmement complexe en laquelle se retrouvent, à doses à peu près égales, les différents types nordiques et méditerranéens. C'est davantage par la langue que par leur type racial que les Belges se distinguent les uns des autres.

Qu'ils soient Flamands ou Wallons, qu'ils parlent le plus volontiers le néerlandais ou le français, voire tel ou tel patois, les Belges se distinguent par une même ardeur au travail, car le peuple belge est d'une vitalité et d'un dynamisme incomparables, et son esprit pratique lui confère un très grand sens des affaires. Il a le goût de la nouveauté et ses possibilités d'assimilation sont infinies.

Si le peuple belge est grand travailleur et s'il peut être économe à ses heures, il n'en est pas moins d'une grande hospitalité, tout comme il possède également le goût du bien vivre et du confort, voire même du luxe. A l'occasion des jours fastes qui rythment le cours de l'année, le peuple belge se montre prodigue de grande liesse, et tant en hiver qu'en été, se succèdent kermesses, ducasses et fêtes de carnaval dont la plupart remontent au moyen âge et connaissent toujours l'affairement des grandes foules. Toutes ces qualités confèrent au Belge une réputation de bon aloi qui le fait aimer et apprécier de quiconque; aussi dans le cœur des étrangers qui l'ont fréquenté occupe-t-il une place de choix, qui est bien souvent la première.

La Belgique est un des plus petits pays de l'Europe, voire même du monde. Elle est située en bordure de la mer du Nord et ses voisins immédiats sont, au nord et au nord-est les Pays-Bas, à l'est l'Allemagne et le Grand-Duché de Luxembourg, et au sud-sud-ouest la France. Sauf dans le sud-est du pays, où l'on rencontre des altitudes ne dépassant cependant pas les 720 m, la Belgique est un pays de plaines et de collines. Elle ne possède que 67 km de côte et la longueur totale de ses frontières ne dépasse guère 1.444 km. La plus grande distance, soit d'Ostende à Arlon, est à peine de 290 km à vol d'oiseau, soit quelque 320 km par la route ou en chemin de fer.

Les richesses du sol et du sous-sol de la Belgique, bien que difficilement comparables à celles des grands états voisins, n'en

Zoals alle volken van Europa vertoont het Belgische volk een zeer ingewikkelde ethnische samenstelling, waarin men, in vrijwel gelijke verhouding, de verschillende Noordse en Mediterrane typen terugvindt. Het is eerder door de taal dan wel door het rassentype, dat de Belgen van elkaar verschillen.

Zowel bij Vlamingen als bij Walen ontdekt men dezelfde werklust. Het Belgische volk bezit immers een onvergelijkelijke levenskracht en dynamisme, en tevens, dank zij zijn gezond verstand en practische geest, een buitengewone aanleg voor de handel. De Belg houdt van nieuwigheden, en zijn assimilatievermogen lijkt haast onbegrensd.

Hoewel het Belgische volk zeer vlijtig is, en op tijd en stond ook zuinig kan zijn, bezit het toch een grote gastvrijheid en toont het veel zin voor goede sier en comfort, ja zelfs voor weelde. Ter gelegenheid van de feestdagen die het jaarverloop ritmeren, kan het Belgische volk zich zeer uitgelaten tonen, en zowel 's winters als tijdens de zomermaanden wisselen kermissen, vastenavondfeesten en dergelijke, waarvan de meeste opklimmen tot in de middeleeuwen, elkaar af, en brengen steeds weer een massa belangstellenden te been. Al deze eigenschappen hebben het Belgische volk een goede reputatie bezorgd. Het wordt door iedereen geacht en gewaardeerd en bekleedt in het hart van de vreemdeling die het van dichtbij kent, een ruime plaats.

België is een van de kleinste landen van Europa en zelfs van de wereld. Het ligt aan de oevers van de Noordzee, en heeft als onmiddellijke buurstaten : in het Noorden en het Noordoosten Nederland, in het Oosten Duitsland en het Groothertogdom Luxemburg en in het Zuid-Zuidwesten Frankrijk. Behalve in het Zuidoosten van het land, waar men hoogten aantreft die echter de 720 meter niet overtreffen, is België een land van laagvlakten en van heuvelen. De kust is slechts 67 km lang, en de totale lengte van zijn grenzen bedraagt ongeveer 1.444 km. De grootste afstand, d.i. van Oostende naar Aarlen, bedraagt in vogelvlucht nauwelijks 290 km (320 km langs de weg of per spoor).

Hoewel de natuurlijke rijkdommen van de grond en van de ondergrond van België moeilijk kunnen vergeleken worden met die van sommige van zijn grote buurlanden, zijn zij nochtans

sont pas moins fort appréciables. L'agriculture et l'élevage se pratiquent partout avec une spécialisation régionale selon la nature du terrain ou en fonction du marché économique. Dans le sous-sol on trouve surtout de la houille, tandis que les carrières de porphyre, de marbre et d'ardoise n'y sont point négligeables.

Quant à la nature des diverses régions de la Belgique, disons qu'elle est multiple et variée, surtout pour une terre aussi exiguë d'à peine quelque 30.507 km². Les paysages y sont sans cesse changeants, depuis ceux en bordure de la mer jusqu'aux hauts plateaux de l'Ardenne et des Fagnes, en passant par de larges zones industrielles qui donnent au pays richesse et prospérité.

En fait la Belgique entière est avant tout une grande ruche laborieuse dont les produits ont conquis depuis longtemps les plus lointains marchés mondiaux, et cela au départ de cinq ports maritimes : Anvers, Gand, Zeebrugge, Ostende et Bruxelles. Anvers en est évidemment le plus réputé, tant en raison de l'excellence de sa situation que de la qualité de son outillage et de sa main-d'œuvre spécialisée.

Notre portrait géographique de la Belgique serait incomplet, si nous ne faisions allusion à la grande densité de sa population, qui est une des premières du monde, avec une moyenne de 290 habitants au km².

Depuis environ un siècle, la population de la Belgique est passée du simple au double, pour compter à l'heure actuelle un peu plus de neuf millions d'habitants. Les trois langues nationales sont le français, le néerlandais et l'allemand, cette dernière langue parlée par quelque 80.000 habitants des cantons de l'est du pays. La Belgique est divisée administrativement en neuf provinces : Anvers, le Brabant, la Flandre Occidentale, la Flandre Orientale, le Hainaut, Liège, le Limbourg, le Luxembourg et Namur; elles sont subdivisées en 41 arrondissements administratifs pour la totalité du territoire et comptent ensemble 2.669 villes et communes.

La plupart des villes belges remontent au moyen âge et trois d'entre elles (Arlon, Tongres et Tournai) datent de l'époque gallo-romaine. Elles conservent en de nombreux monuments historiques, de même que dans la physionomie de leurs rues et de leurs places publiques, la trace de cette origine lointaine, mais depuis la fin du siècle dernier, elles se sont modernisées à un rythme accéléré, de telle sorte que les grandes villes belges comptent actuellement parmi les cités les plus modernes de la vieille Europe.

niet te onderschatten. Landbouw en veeteelt worden zowat overal beoefend, maar vertonen bepaalde gewestelijke kenmerken of specialisaties al naar gelang de aard van de bodem of van de afzetmogelijkheden. Ondergronds worden vooral steenkolen gewonnen, terwijl ook de porfier-, marmer- en leisteengroeven niet onbelangrijk zijn.

Het wezen en uitzicht van de verschillende Belgische streken is even rijk als verscheiden, wat eerder verrassend is voor een land met een oppervlakte van ternauwernood 30.507 km². De landschappen volgen op elkaar in grote verscheidenheid, van de zeekust tot de hoogvlakten van de Ardennen en van de Hoge Venen, via uitgestrekte nijverheidsstreken, die een bron van rijkdom en voorspoed vormen.

In werkelijkheid gelijkt België vooral op een bedrijvige bijenkorf, waarvan de produkten sedert lang, via vijf zeehavens : Antwerpen, Gent, Zeebrugge, Oostende en Brussel naar de verste wereldmarkten worden uitgevoerd. Daarvan is Antwerpen vanzelfsprekend de meest vermaarde, dank zij haar uitstekende ligging, haar voortreffelijke uitrusting en haar gespecialiseerde arbeiders.

Dit geografische overzicht van België zou zeker onvolledig zijn, wanneer wij er niet de Belgische bevolkingsdichtheid bij betrokken, die nagenoeg 290 inwoners per km² bedraagt en een der grootste ter wereld is.

Sedert ongeveer een eeuw is de bevolking van België verdubbeld, zodat zij thans de 9 miljoen inwoners overtreft. De drie nationale talen zijn het Nederlands, het Frans en het Duits; deze laatste is de moedertaal van ongeveer 80.000 inwoners in de oostelijke kantons van de provincie Luik.

Op administratief gebied is België verdeeld in negen provinciën : Antwerpen, Brabant, Oost-Vlaanderen, West-Vlaanderen, Henegouwen, Luik, Limburg, Luxemburg en Namen; zij zijn onderverdeeld in 41 bestuursarrondissementen voor het gehele grondgebied, dat verder 2.669 steden en gemeenten telt.

De oorsprong van de meeste Belgische steden reikt tot de Middeleeuwen, en drie ervan (Aarlen, Tongeren en Doornik) dagtekenen zelfs uit het Gallo-Romeinse tijdvak. De sporen van deze verre oorsprong kan men nog terugvinden, niet alleen in talrijke historische monumenten, maar ook in de rooilijn van straten en pleinen in de oude stadsgedeelten; sedert het einde van de vorige eeuw hebben zij zich echter in versneld tempo gemoderniseerd, zodat de grote Belgische steden op dit ogenblik tot de modernste van het oude Europa behoren.

The Belgians
and their small country
on the shore of the North sea

Das Belgische Volk
und das Land
an der Nordsee

Like all the European populations, the Belgian people are a highly complex ethnic group composed, in almost equal parts, of the various nordic and mediterranean groups. They differ form each other by their languages, rather than by racial features.

Whether they are Flemings or Walloons, and speak preferably Dutch or French, or even one of the dialects, the Belgians, in their hard work, display considerable vitality and drive. They are pragmatic, and excellent business people. They like innovations, and possess an unlimited adaptability.

These hard workers who can be thrifty also are very hospitable. They like the good life, comfort, and even luxury. Festive occasions mark the course of the year, and the population takes a full part in the funfairs, celebrations and carnivals, both in Winter and in Summer. Most of these festivities originated in the Middle Ages, and draw large crowds. The Belgian is an easy-going, likeable fellow; the foreigner who gets to know him appreciates him, sometimes more than others.

Belgium is one of the smallest countries in Europe and in the world. It is located on the North Sea, its immediate neighbourgs being the Netherlands in the North and North-East, Germany and the Grand Duchy of Luxembourg in the East, and France in the South-South-West. Except for the South-East of the country, where there are heights of up to 720 m above sea-level, Belgium is a country of plains and hills. Its coast has an overall length of a mere 67 km, and the sum total of its borders does not exceed 444 km. The greatest distance, from Ostend to Arlon, totals 290 km as the crow flies, or some 320 km by road or train.

Belgium's resources in its soil and subsoil, while hardly comparable to those of its large neighbouring states, are not negligible.

Farming and stock-breeding are practiced everywhere, in specialized farms according to the nature of the soil, or the

Wie alle europäischen Völker hat das belgische Volk eine sehr verwickelte ethnische Zusammensetzung, in der man in beinahe gleichmässigen Verhältnissen die verschiedenen Nordsee- und Mittelmeertypen wiederfindet. Die Sprache ist es, wodurch die Belgier verschieden sind.

Bei Flamen und Wallonen entdeckt man dieselbe Arbeitsfreude; denn das belgische Volk besitzt viel dynamische Lebenskraft. Durch seinen gesunden Verstand und seinen praktischen Geist ist es geradezu vorbestimmt für den Handel. Der Belgier liebt Neuigkeiten und seine Anpassungsfähigkeit scheint beinahe unbegrenzt. Obwohl das belgische Volk sehr fleissig ist und zeitweilig sparsam sein kann, ist es dabei sehr gastfrei und gönnt es sich selbst gern was, liebt Komfort, ja selbst Üppigkeit. Anlässlich von Festtagen kann der Belgier sehr ausgelassen sein. Im Winter wie im Sommer folgen Kirmessen, Fastnachtfeste und dergleichen aufeinander, deren Ursprung oftmals bis ins Mittelalter zurückreicht. Diese Feste bringen immer wieder grosse Menschenmengen auf die Beine. Alle diese Eigenschaften haben dem belgischen Volk einen guten Ruf verschafft. Es wird von allen geachtet und geschätzt. Die Herzen der Fremden, die es näher kennen, nimmt es sehr für sich ein.

Belgien ist eines der kleinsten Länder Europas, ja selbst der Welt. Es erstreckt sich an der Nordseeküste und seine unmittelbare Nachbarn sind im Nord-Nordosten Holland, im Osten Deutschland und das Grossherzogtum Luxemburg und im Süd-Südwesten Frankreich. Ausser im Südosten des Landes, wo es Berge gibt, die jedoch 720 m nicht übersteigen, ist Belgien ein Land von Tiefebenen und Hügeln. Die Küste ist nur 67 km lang, und die totale Länge seiner Grenzen beträgt ungefähr 1.444 km. Der grösste Abstand, von Ostende nach Arlon, beträgt in der Luftlinie kaum 290 km, 320 km auf der Landstrasse oder per Eisenbahn.

Obwohl die natürlichen Reichtümer des Bodens und Untergrundes sich nur schwer mit denen von einigen der grossen Nachbarstaaten vergleichen lassen, sind sie doch nicht zu unterschätzen. Ackerbau und Viehzucht werden überall ausgeübt, doch sind sie gekennzeichnet durch bestimmte landschaftliche

requirements of the market. The subsoil's main resource is coal; porphyry, marmor, and slate also are being quarried in substantial quantities.

The landscape in the regions of the country varies continuously, a striking characteristic since its overall surface does not exceed 30,507 km². The features change constantly from the flat plain along the sea-coast to the high plateaus of the Ardennes and Fagnes, with, in-between, large industrial areas that provide for the country's progress and prosperity.

Belgium, in fact, is, in the first place, a busy bee-hive whose products, dispatched from its five sea-ports—Antwerp, Ghent, Zeebrugge, Ostend and Brussels—are well-established on the world's markets. Antwerp is the better-known one, because of its excellent location, its first-class equipment, and highly qualified labour.

Our geographical picture of Belgium has yet another dimension: the density of its population. The average of 290 inhabitants per square km ranks it among the highest populated in the world.

In approximately one century, Belgium's population has doubled; the figure, today, is slightly over nine millions. The three national languages are French, Dutch and German, the latter being spoken by some 80,000 people in the Eastern districts. Belgium is divided, administratively, in nine provinces: Antwerp, Brabant, West Flanders, East Flanders, Hainaut, Liège, Limburg, Luxembourg and Namur. Each of them is subdivided in administrative districts, totalling 41 for the country as a whole. Together, they total 2,669 cities and communes.

Most Belgian cities were created in the Middle Ages. Three of them—Arlon, Tongeren and Tournai—were founded in Gallo-Roman times. They have many historic monuments and the lay-out of their streets and market places reveals their ancient origin. Since the end of the previous century, however, they have been thoroughly modernized. Today, Belgium's big cities rank among the most modern ones in ancient Europe.

Verschiedenheit nach Art des Bodens oder der Absatzmöglichkeiten. Im Boden findet sich vor allem Steinkohle, während auch die Porphyr-, Marmor- und Schiefergruben nicht unbedeutend sind. Die Landschaft Belgiens ist sehr reich und abwechslungsvoll, besonders wenn man bedenkt, dass die Oberfläche des Landes kaum 30.507 qkm beträgt.

Von der Seeküste bis zu den Hochebenen der Ardennen und dem Hohen Venn, über ausgebreitete Industriegebiete, die eine Quelle von Reichtum und Wohlstand sind, folgen vielfältige Landschaften aufeinander.

Belgien ähnelt auffallend einem emsigen Bienenvolk, dessen Produkte seit langem über fünf Seehäfen : Antwerpen, Gent, Zeebrügge, Oostende und Brüssel, zu den fernsten Weltmärkten ausgeführt werden. Von diesen Häfen ist Antwerpen der bedeutendste, wegen seiner guten Lage sowohl wie wegen seiner hervorragenden Ausstattung und seiner spezialisierten Arbeiter.

Diese geografische Übersicht von Belgien wäre unvollständig, wenn man nicht auf die Dichtheit seiner Bevölkerung hinwiese, die nahezu 290 Einwohner per qkm beträgt und damit beinahe die grösste der Welt ist.

Seit einem Jahrhundert hat sich die Bevölkerung Belgiens verdoppelt, so dass sie jetzt 9½ Millionen übertrifft. Die drei Landessprachen sind Niederländisch, Französisch und Deutsch. Deutsch ist die Muttersprache von ca 80.000 Einwohnern in den östlichen Kantonen der Provinz Lüttich.

Verwaltungsmässig ist Belgien in neun Provinzen eingeteilt : Antwerpen, Brabant, Hainaut, Ostflandern, Westflandern, Lüttich, Limburg, Luxemburg und Namur. Sie sind in 41 Regierungsbezirke über das ganze Grundgebiet unterteilt, das 2.669 Städte und Dörfer zählt.

Der Ursprung der meisten belgischen Städte reicht bis in das Mittelalter zurück, und verschiedene unter ihnen (u.a. Arlon, Tongeren, Tournai) datieren selbst aus der gallo-römischen Zeit. Die Spuren dieses fernen Ursprungs findet man noch in zahlreichen historischen Monumenten, auch in der »Richtlinie« von Strassen und Plätzen in den alten Stadtteilen. Seit dem Ende des vorigen Jahrhunderts haben die Städte sich jedoch in einem derart schnellen Tempo modernisiert, dass sie in diesem Augenblick zu den modernsten des alten Europas gehören.

1. Bruxelles. La tour de l'hôtel de ville, haute de 90 m. (15ᵉ s.) – Brussel. De negentig meter hoge toren van het stadhuis (15de e.) – Brussels. The town hall-tower, height 90 m. (15th c.) – Brüssel. Der Rathausturm, 90 m. hoch (15. Jh). *Photo: F. van den Bremt*

2. Bruxelles. Notre-Dame du Sablon (15ᵉ-16ᵉ s.) – Brussel.
O.-L.-Vrouw van de Zavel (15de-16de e.) – Brussels. Our Lady
of the Sablon (15th-16th c.) – Brüssel. Sablonkirche (15.-16. Jh).
Photo: archives

3. Bruxelles. Grand'Place, maisons des corporations (fin 17ᵉ s.) –
Brussel. Grote Markt, gildehuizen (eind 17de e.) – Brussels.
Grand'Place, guild houses (end 17th c.) – Brüssel. Grand'Place,
Zunfthäuser (E. 17. Jh). *Photo: F. van den Bremt*

5. Bruxelles. L'hôtel de ville la nuit, vue du Mont des Arts – Brussel. Het stadhuis bij nacht, gezien vanaf de Kunstberg – Brussels. The town hall by night, seen from the Mont des Arts – Brüssel. Das Rathaus bei Nacht, gesehen vom Mont des Arts. *Photo: C.G.T., Esterhazy*

◀ 4. Bruxelles. Manneken-Pis, œuvre de J. Duquesnoy (17ᵉ s.) – Brussel. Manneken-Pis, werk van J. Duquesnoy (17de e.) – Brussels Manneken-Pis « oldest citizen of Brussels » by J. Duquesnoy (17th c.) – Brüssel. Manneken-Pis « der älteste Einwohner der Stadt » von J. Duquesnoy (17. Jh). *Photo: archives*

◀ **6.** Bruxelles. Tour de la cathédrale St-Michel (15ᵉ s.) – Brussel. Toren van de St-Michielskathedraal (15de e.) – Brussels. Tower of the cathedral of St-Michael (15th c.) – Brüssel. Turm der St-Michaelskathedrale (15. Jh). *Photo: archives*

7. Beersel. Le château féodal restauré (14ᵉ s.) – **Het gerestaureerde middeleeuwse kasteel (14de e.) .– The restored feudal castle (14th c.) – Das restaurierte feudale Schloß (14. Jh).** *Photo: C.G.T., Esterhazy*

8. Halle. Grand'Place et basilique Not
Dame (14ᵉ s.) – Grote markt en O.-
Vrouwbasiliek (14de e.) – Grand'Pl
and Basilica Notre-Dame (14th c.)
Marktplatz und Liebfrauenkirche (
Jh). *Photo: F. van den Bremt*

9. Grimbergen. L'église abbatiale (17ᵉ s.), intérieur – De abdijkerk
(17de e.), binnengezicht – The abbey church (17th c.), interior
– Die Abteikirche (17. Jh). *Photo: Prov. Brabant*

11. Villers-la-Ville. Ruines de l'abbaye cistercienne (1146) – Ruïnen van de cisterciënseradbij (1146) – Ruins of the cistercian abbey (1146) – Ruïnen der Zisterzienserabtei (1146). *Photo: C.G.T., Tas*

◀ **10.** Groot-Bijgaarden. L'entrée du château (17ᵉ s.) – Toegang tot het kasteel (17de e.) – Entry of the castle (17th c.) – Die Schloß-pforte (17. Jh). *Photo: C.G.T., De Meyer*

13. Waterloo. La ferme historique « la Haie Sainte » – De historische hoeve « la Haie Sainte » – The historical farm « la Haie Sainte » – Der historischer Hof « la Haie Sainte ». *Photo: C.G.T.*

12. Nivelles L'église Ste-Gertrude (11ᵉ-13ᵉ s.) – De St-Geertrui-kerk (11de-13de e.) – St-Gertrude collegiate church (11th-13th c.) – St-Gertrudiskirche (11.-13. Jh). *Photo: archives*

14. Waterloo. La butte et le lion – De heuvel en de leeuw – The Lion hill – Der Löwenhügel. *Photo: C.G.T., L. Philippe*

16. Gaasbeek. Le château féodal – Het middeleeuwse kasteel –
The feudal castle – Das feudale Schloß. *Photo: C.G.T., Demeyer*

◀ **15.** Leuven. L'hôtel de ville (15ᵉ s.) – Het stadhuis (15de e.) –
The town hall (15th c.) – Das Rathaus (15. Jh). *Photo: C.G.T.,
Dierickx*

17. Leuven. Le béguinage
(14ᵉ s.) – Het begijnhof
(14de e.) – The beguinage
(14th c.) – Der Beginenhof
(14. Jh). *Photo: F. van der Bremt*

18. Zoutleeuw. L'église gothique (13ᵉ s.) — De gotische kerk
(13de e.) — The gothic church (13th c.) — Die gotische Kirche
(13. Jh). *Photo: C.G.T., Esterhazy*

19. Diest. Église St-Sulpice, détail (15e s.) — St-Sulpitius, detail (15de e.) — Church St-Sulpice (15th c.) — St-Sulpitiuskirche (15. Jh). *Photo: F. van den Bremt*

20. Diest. Entrée du béguinage – Hoofdtoegang van het begijnhof
– Entry of the beguinâge – Haupteingang des Beginenhofes.
Photo: C.G.T.

22. Tervuren. Le musée de l'Afrique centrale – Het museum van Centraal-Afrika – The museum of Central Africa – Das Museum von Zentral-Afrika. *Photo: Prov. Brabant*

◀ **21.** Hakendover. Détail du retable sculpté (vers 1400) – Detail van het gebeeldhouwde retabel (ca 1400) – Detail of the carved altarpiece (about 1400) – Teil des geschnitzten Altars (um 1400). *Photo: A.C.L.*

23. Scherpenheuvel. La basilique (1605) – De basiliek (1605) –
The basilica (1605) – Die Liebfrauenkirche (1605). *Photo: archives*

24. Mons. Le singe « del Grand Garde » – Bronzen aapje « del Grand Garde » – Monkey of the Big Guard – Der bronzene Affe « del Grand Garde ». *Photo: C.G.T.*

26. Tournai. Le marché, la cathédrale (12ᵉ-13ᵉ s.), le beffroi
(12ᵉ s.) – De markt, de kathedraal (12de-13de e.), het belfort
(12de e.) – Market-place, cathedral (12th-13th c.), belfry (12th c.)
– Marktplatz, Kathedrale (12.-13. Jh), und Belfried (12. Jh).
Photo: C.G.T., Esterhazy

◀ **25.** Mons. Le beffroy (17ᵉ s.) – Het belfort (17de e.) – The Belfry
(17th c.) – Der Belfried (17. Jh). *Photo: C.G.T.*

28. Belœil. Le château des princes de Ligne (18ᵉ-20ᵉ s.) – Het kasteel der prinsen de Ligne (18de-20ste e.) – The castle of the princes de Ligne (18th-20th c.) – Das Schloß der Fürsten de Ligne (18.-20. Jh). *Photo: C.G.T., L. Philippe*

◀ **27.** Tournai. Jubé de la cathédrale (16ᵉ s.) – Doksaal van de kathedraal (16de e.) – Rood-screen of the cathedral (16th c.) – Lettner der Kathedrale (16. Jh). *Photo: archives*

◀ **29.** Binche. Gille. *Photo: C.G.T.*

30. Hollain. Menhir « La pierre Brunehaut » (préhistorique) – Menhir « La pierre Brunehaut » (voorhistorisch) – Menhir « La pierre Brunehaut » (prehistoric) – Menhir « La pierre Brunehaut » (vorgeschichtlich). *Photo: C.G.T., Mathieu*

32. Le pays noir. La Sambre à Montignies – Het zwarte land.
De Samber te Montignies – The black country. The Sambre at
Montignies – Das schwarze Land. Die Sambre zu Montignies.
Photo: C.G.T.

31. Aulne. Ruines de l'abbaye (13ᵉ-18ᵉ s.) – Puinen van de abdij
(13de-18de e.) – Ruins of the Abbey (13th-18th c.) – Ruinen der
Abtei (13.-18. Jh). *Photo: C.G.T.*

33. Gent. Le Rabot (fin 15ᵉ s.) – Het Rabot (eind 15de e.) –
The Rabot (end of the 15th c.) – Das Rabot (Ende des 15. Jh).
Photo: C.G.T.

34. Gent. Le château des comtes (12ᵉ s.) – Het gravenkasteel (12de e.) – Castle of the counts (12th c.) – Das Grafenschloß (12. Jh). *Photo: C.G.T., Esterhazy*

35. Gent. Les trois tours (St-Nicolas, beffroi, St-Michel) – De drie torens (St-Niklaas, belfort, en St-Michiels) – The three towers (St-Nicholas, belfry and St-Michael) – Die drei Türme (St-Nikolaus, Belfried und St-Michael). *Photo: C.G.T.*

36. Gent. Les quais, maisons anciennes – De Graskaai, oude huizen – The quays, old houses – Alte Häuser am Kai. *Photo: archives*

38. Bachte-Maria-Leerne. Le château Ooidonck – Het kasteel Ooidonck – The castle Ooidonck – Das Schloß Ooidonck. *Photo: C.G.T., A. De Belder*

◀ **37.** Drongen. L'ancienne abbaye (17ᵉ s.) – De voormalige abdij (17de e.) – The ancient abbey (17th c.) – Die alte Abtei (17. Jh). *Photo: Sabena*

39. Paysage scaldien – Scheldelandschap – Scheldtlandscape – Scheldelandschaft. *Photo: archives*

40. Temse. Panorama. *Photo: C.G.T.*

43. Ronse. Crypte romane de l'église St-Hermes (11ᵉ s.) – Romaanse krocht van de St-Hermeskerk (11de e.) – Romanesque crypt of St-Hermes (11th c.) – Romanische Krypte der St-Hermes-kirche (11. Jh). *Photo: C.G.T., Sergijsels*

44. Oudenaarde. L'hôtel de ville (16ᵉ s.) – Stadhuis (16de e.) – Town hall (16th c.) – Rathaus (16. Jh). *Photo: C.G.T., L. Philippe*

45. Brugge. Tour de l'église Notre-Dame – Toren van de O.-L.-Vrouwkerk – Tower of the Notre-Dame church – Turm der Liebfrauenkirche. *Photo: archives*

46. Brugge. Un des canaux pittoresques – Een der schilderachtige reien – One of the picturesque canals – Einer der malerischen Kanäle. *Photo: C.G.T.*

47. Brugge. La procession du Saint-Sang – Tafereel uit de H. Bloed-processie – The Holy Blood procession – Die H. Blutprozession.
Photo: C.G.T., Buyle

48. Lissewege. L'église gothique (13ᵉ s.) – De gotische kerk (13de e.) – Gothic church (13th c.) – Die gotische Kirche (13. Jh).
Photo: C.G.T., Esterhazy

49. Brugge. Quai du Rosaire – De Rozenhoedkaai – The Rosary Quay – Der Rosenhutkai. *Photo: C.G.T., Sergijsels*

50. Damme. Paysage et panorama – Landschap en panorama – The country-side and panorama – Landschaft und Panorama. *Photo: C.G.T., Halsberghe*

◀ **51.** Les polders maritimes – De zeepolders – Polder landscape –
Polderlandschaft. *Photo: C.G.T., De Meyer*

52. Damme. L'hôtel de ville (15ᵉ s.) – Stadhuis (15de e.) – Town
hall (15th c.) – Rathaus (15. Jh). *Photo: C.G.T., Esterhazy*

54. Ieper. Fanfare folklorique devant les Halles (13ᵉ s.) – **Folkloristische fanfare voor de Hallen (13de e.)** – Folkloric fanfare in front of the cloth hall (13th c.) – **Folkloristische Fanfare vor den Hallen (13. Jh).** *Photo: C.G.T., Esterhazy*

◀ **53.** Ieper. « Kattefeest ». *Photo: C.G.T., Buyle*

55. Veurne. Panorama. *Photo: C.G.T.*

56. Kortrijk. Le béguinage (13e s.) – Het begijnhof (13de e.) –
The beguinage (13th c.) – Der Beginenhof (13. Jh). *Photo: C.G.T.,*
Esterhazy

57. Paysage près de Bruges – Landschap in de omgeving van
Brugge – Landscape near Bruges – Landschaft in der Umgebung
von Brügge. *Photo: C.G.T.*

58. Champ de lin en Flandre – Vlasveld in Vlaanderen – Flaxfield in Flanders – Flachsfeld in Flandern. *Photo: C.G.T.*

59. Oostende. Les plaisirs de la plage – Strandgenoegens – The pleasures of the beach – Strandvergnügen. *Photo: C.G.T., De Meyer*

60. La côte belge : les dunes, la plage et la mer – De Belgische kust : zee, strand en duinen – The Belgian coast : sea, beach and dunes – Die belgische Küste : Meer, Strand und Dünen. *Photo: C.G.T., Esterhazy*

61. Pêcheur aux crevettes – Garnaalvisser – Shrimp fisherman –
Garnalenfischer. *Photo: C.G.T., Ramelot*

62. Nieuwpoort. Bâteaux de pêche – Vissersboten – Fishing-boats
– Fischerbote. *Photo: C.G.T., L. Philippe*

63. Lissewege. Grange monumentale de l'abbaye Ter Doest
(13ᵉ s.) – Monumentale schuur van de abdij Ter Doest (13de e.) –
Monumental barn of the abbey Ter Doest (13th c.) – Monumentale
Scheune der Abtei Ter Doest (13. Jh). *Photo: A.C.L.*

64. Oostende. Le môle – De pier – The mole – Der Mole.
Photo: C.G.T.

65. Liège. Cour du palais des princes-évêques (16ᵉ s.) – Ereplein van het Prinsbisschoppelijk paleis (16de e.) – Courtyard of the palace of the Prince Bishops (16th c.) – Innenhof des Palastes der Prinz-Bischöfe. *Photo: archives*

66. Liège. Le perron, œuvre de Jean Del Cour (17ᵉ s.) – Het perron, werk van Jean Del Cour (17de e.) – The perron, masterpiece of Jean Del Cour (17th c.) – Der « Perron », Meisterwerk von Jean Del Cour (17. Jh). *Photo: C.G.T.*

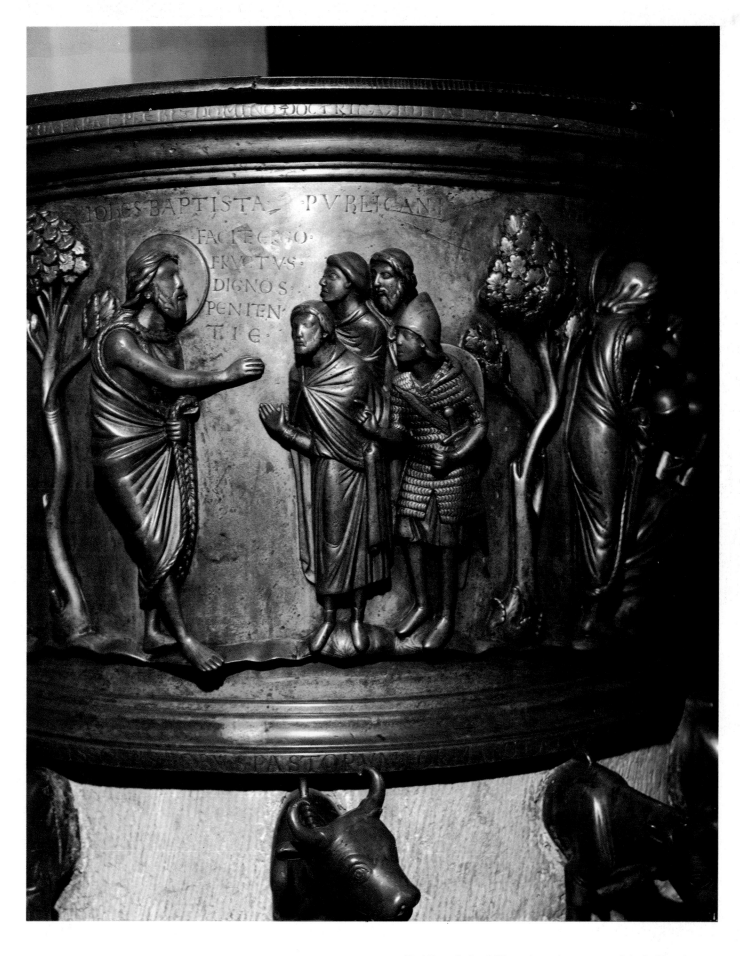

Within the relief, the following inscriptions appear:

...OJES BAPTISTA PVBLICAN...

FAC IE ERGO
FRVCTVS
DIGNOS
PENITEN
TIE

...PASTORVM...

◀ 67. Liège. La maison Curtius (Renaissance mosane) – Het Curtius-
huis (Maaslandse renaissance) – The Curtius mansion (Meuse
renaissance) – Das Curtiushaus (Renaissance). Photo: C.G.T., Dédé

68. Liège. St-Barthélémy, fonts baptismaux. Détail (12ᵉ s.)
St-Bartholomeus, doopvont. Detail (12de e.) – St-Bartholomew,
baptismal fonts (12th c.) – St-Bartholomäus, Taufbecken (12. Jh).
Photo: C.G.T.

70. Spa. Panorama. *Photo: C.G.T., Esterhazy*

◀ **69.** Stavelot. « Les Blancs Moussis ». *Photo C.G.T., L. Philippe*

71. Eupen. Carnaval – Karnaval – Carnival – Karneval. *Photo: C.G.T., Robelus*

72. Modave. Le château (18ᵉ s.) – Het kasteel (18de e.) – **The castle** (18th c.) – Das Schloß (18. Jh). *Photo: C.G.T.*

73. Huy. Collégiale Notre-Dame, portail de Bethléhem (13ᵉ s.) – O.-L.-Vrouwkerk, „ Bethlehem ”-portaal (13de e.) – Notre-Dame church, Bethlehem portico (13th c.) – Die Liebfrauen-kirche, Bethlehemportal (13. Jh). *Photo: archives*

74. Huy. L'hôtel de ville et la fontaine dite « bassinia » (1406) – Het stadhuis en « bassinia »-fontein (1406) – The townhall and the fountain « bassinia » (1406) – Das Rathaus und der « Bassinia »-Brunnen (1406). *Photo: C.G.T.*

75. Namur. Cathédrale St-Aubin (Baroque) – St-Aubinkathedraal
(Barok) – Cathedral of St-Aubin (Baroque) – Kathedrale St-Aubin
(Barock). *Photo: archives*

76. Namur. Panorama. *Photo: C.G.T., Esterhazy*

78. Dinant. Le rocher Bayard, monolythe de 40 m. de hauteur – De Bayardrots, een 40 m. hoge monoliet – The Bayard-rock, 130 feet high monolith – Der Bayard-Felsen, 40 m. hoher Monolyth. *Photo: C.G.T.*

81. Les Hautes Fagnes – De Hoge Venen – The « Hautes Fagnes »
– Das Hohe Venn. *Photo: archives*

82. Spontin. Ancien château féodal – Oud feodaal slot – Ancient feudal castle – Mittelalterliches Schloß. *Photo: C.G.T., L. Philippe*

84. Mazy. Ferme fortifiée – Versterkte hoeve – Fortified farm –
Befestigter Bauernhof. *Photo: C.G.T., Esterhazy*

◀ **83.** Grupont. Maison construite en colombage – Huis in vakwerk-
bouw – House in timberwork – Haus in Fachwerkbau. *Photo:
C.G.T., De Meyer*

85. Dohan-sur-Semois. Le village – Het dorp – The village –
Das Dorf. *Photo: C.G.T., De Sutter*

86. Bastogne. Le monument de la liberté – Het vrijheidsmonument – The liberty monument – Das Freiheitsdenkmal. *Photo:* *C.G.T., Esterhazy*

87. Botassart. Le tombeau du géant — Het graf van de reus —
The tomb of the giant — Grabstätte des Riesen. *Photo: archives*

88. Virton. Le musée Gaumais – Museum van de Gaume – Museum « Gaumais » – Das Museum der Gaume. *Photo: C.G.T., Esterhazy*

90. Sint-Truiden. Grand'Place, hôtel de ville (14ᵉ s.) et beffroi, tour de l'ancienne abbaye (11ᵉ s.) et église Notre-Dame (14ᵉ s.) – Grote markt, stadhuis (14de e.) en belfort, toren van de voormalige abdij (11de e.) en O.L. Vrouwkerk (14de e.) – Grand' Place, town hall (14th c.) and belfry, tower of the abbey (11th c.) and collegiate N.-D. (14th c.) – Marktplatz, Rathaus (14. Jh.) und Belfried, Abteiturm (11. Jh) und Liebfrauenkirche (14. Jh.). *Photo: C.G.T., L. Philippe*

91. Bokrijk. Musée en plein air – Openluchtmuseum – Open-air museum – Freiluftmuseum. *Photo: F. van den Bremt*

92. Tongeren. Basilique Notre-Dame (13ᵉ-16ᵉ s.) et statue
d'Ambiorix – O.-L.-Vrouwbasiliek (13de-16de e.) en standbeeld
van Ambiorix – Notre-Dame basilica (13th-16th c.) and statue
of Ambiorix – Liebfrauenkirche (13.-16. Jh) und Denkmal des
Ambiorix. *Photo: C.G.T., J. Marlier*

93. Tongeren. Cloître roman – Romaans kloosterpand – Romanesque cloisters – Romanischer Kreuzgang. *Photo: archives*

94. Antwerpen. Place de l'hôtel de ville : hôtel de ville (16ᵉ s.),
maisons des corporations et fontaine – Grote markt, stadhuis
(16de e.), gildehuizen en Brabofontein – Town hall square,
town hall (16th c.), guild houses and fountain – Rathausplatz,
Rathaus (16. Jh) Zunfthäuser und Brunnen. *Photo: C.G.T., Tas*

96. Antwerpen. Une des multiples chapelles mariales – Een der
vele typisch Antwerpse Mariabeeldjes – One of the numerous
devotional chapels – Eins der vielen typischen Antwerpener
Mariabilder. *Photo: C.G.T., Tas*

97. Antwerpen. Le port – De haven – The harbour – Der See-
hafen. *Photo: F. van den Bremt*

98. Lier. L'hôtel de ville (18ᵉ s.) et le beffroi – Stadhuis (18de e.) en belfort – Town hall (18th c.) and belfry – Rathaus (16. Jh) und Belfried. *Photo: C.G.T., L. Philippe*

99. Mechelen. Tour de la cathédrale St-Rombout – Toren van de St-Romboutskathedraal – Tower of St-Rombout – Turm der St-Rombalduskathedrale. *Photo: F. van den Bremt*

100. Mechelen. Hôtel de ville et ancien palais de Marguerite d'Autriche (16ᵉ s.) – Stadhuis en voormalig paleis van Margareta van Oostenrijk (16de e.) – Town hall and former palace of Margaret of Austria (16th c.) – Rathaus und Palast der Margareta von Österreich (16. Jh). *Photo: C.G.T., Esterhazy*

101. Mechelen. Vieille maison au Quai au Sel – Oud huis aan de
Zoutkaai – Old house along de Quai au Sel – Altes Haus am
Salzkai. *Photo: F. van den Bremt*

LE VISAGE DES VILLES ET DES SITES BELGES

Une évocation de la Belgique, sans une courte description de ses principaux centres et sites naturels, nous paraîtrait chose vraiment incomplète, car pour les voyageurs belges aussi bien que pour les visiteurs étrangers, ce qui se présente d'abord à leur attention ou plutôt à leur émerveillement, c'est le visage extérieur des villes et des paysages, avec leurs attraits immédiats, leurs beautés naturelles et leurs monuments historiques.

Ce visage extérieur, ce visage touristique, comme on a l'habitude de l'appeler depuis la multiplication et la démocratisation des voyages, est pour la Belgique un visage plein de grâces multiples et sans cesse changeantes. Impossible, en effet, de faire, en ce petit pays, quelques kilomètres sans rencontrer un village recélant au moins un joyau d'art, vestige de son prestigieux passé. Impossible également de faire plus de trente ou quarante kilomètres, sans voir changer les aspects du paysage, de telle sorte que le voyageur, qui parcourt, par exemple, la Belgique d'Ostende, capitale du littoral belge, jusqu'à Verviers, grand centre drapier à quelque 20 km de la frontière allemande, aura l'impression de voir se dérouler, devant ses yeux émerveillés, une véritable synthèse de ce que l'Europe peut lui offrir de plus beau et de plus varié.

Il y a d'abord la mer du Nord et ses plages de sable fin, ses cités balnéaires et ses dunes. A peine a-t-on dépassé ces dunes, qu'apparaissent les polders, terres basses aux innombrables rangées de peupliers inclinés par les vents du grand large. Au bout de quelque 20 km voici Bruges, l'incomparable cité médiévale, surnommée la Venise du Nord, où l'on pourrait s'arrêter durant des jours; mais le voyage se poursuivant, nous voici, après 50 km, aux abords de Gand, sa cité sœur dans les fastes de l'histoire du comté de Flandre. Déjà, le paysage a changé d'aspect à deux ou trois reprises : aux plaines ont succédé des ondulations peut-être encore molles, mais ce n'est déjà plus la plaine.

Nous venons de dépasser Alost; encore quelques kilomètres et voici les collines brabançonnes. Au loin, pointe le dôme du palais de justice de Bruxelles. Mais nous contournerons la capitale pour poursuivre notre route, d'abord en direction de Louvain, avec ses joyaux d'art, ensuite, à travers les plaines de la

STEDEN EN LANDSCHAPPEN

Een overzicht als dit van België, zonder de bondige beschrijving van de voornaamste toeristische centra en landschappen, lijkt ons onvolledig. Immers, zowel de Belgische reiziger als de buitenlandse bezoeker, wordt in de eerste plaats getroffen door de aanblik van steden en landschappen, met hun opvallende charme, hun natuurlijke schoonheid en hun historische monumenten.

Dit uiterlijke beeld, dit toeristische beeld, zoals men het noemt sedert de vulgarisatie en de democratisering van het reizen, vertoont voor België veelvuldige, voortdurend wisselende bekoorlijkheden. Het is in dit kleine land onmogelijk enige weg af te leggen zonder een stad of dorp te ontmoeten, waar niet een kostbaar kunstwerk uit zijn roemrijk verleden wordt bewaard. Het is evenmin mogelijk 30 of 40 kilometer af te leggen, zonder het landschap te zien veranderen. De reiziger die België doorkruist van Oostende, de hoofdplaats van de Belgische kust, tot Verviers, het centrum van de lakenweverij op ongeveer 20 km van de Duitse grens, krijgt de indruk een ware synthese te beleven van wat Europa aan schoonheid en verscheidenheid bezit.

Er is vooreerst de Noordzee met haar strand van fijn zand, haar badplaatsen en duinen. Nauwelijks heeft men de duinen achter zich, of daar verschijnen de polders, een opeenvolging van lage landen met ontelbare rijen populieren, die de heersende zeewinden landwaarts doen hellen. Op ongeveer 20 km ligt Brugge, het Venetië van het Noorden, de onvergelijkelijke middeleeuwse stad, waar men dagenlang zou kunnen vertoeven. Wij moeten echter onze reis voortzetten, en na 50 km bereiken wij de buitenwijken van Gent, de zusterstad van Brugge in het glorierijke verleden van het graafschap Vlaanderen. Ondertussen is het landschap twee- of driemaal van uitzicht veranderd: de vlakte heeft plaats gemaakt voor lichte golvingen.

Wij hebben nu Aalst achter de rug en na enkele kilometers zien wij de Brabantse heuvelruggen opdagen. In de verte verheft zich de koepel van het Brusselse justitiepaleis. Wij rijden de hoofdstad voorbij om onze reis voort te zetten, eerst in de richting van Leuven, met haar talrijke kunstschatten, en vervol-

ASPECTS OF THE BELGIAN TOWNS AND LANDSCAPES

A notice on Belgium needs to be completed by a short description of its main centres and landscapes. Both, Belgian travellers and foreign tourists are, in the first place, confronted with, and charmed by, the features of the cities and landscapes, with their immediate appeal, their natural beauty and their historic monuments.

Belgium's assets for tourism—increasingly important in an age of intensive and democratic travelling—are numerous and highly diversified. One cannot travel over a few miles in this small country without reaching a village with at least one work of art that recalls a glorious past. One cannot progress over some twenty or thirty miles without noticing a complete change in the landscape. As he travels, say, from Ostend, capital of the Belgian sea-coast, to Verviers, the great textile centre some 15 miles from the German border, the tourist will view a real synthesis of all the various beauties Europe can offer.

First, there is the North Sea, with its beaches of fine sand, its seaside resorts and its dunes. Beyond the dunes are the polders—sunk-meadows with numerous rows of poplars bent by the sea-breeze. Some 15 miles further, there is Brugge, the superb mediaeval city, also called the Venice of the North, where one could spend several days. As one progresses further, one reaches, after some 35 miles, Ghent, the famous historical sister-city of the County of Flanders. The landscape has already changed a couple of times. The flat fields have been replaced by some slight undulations.

A few miles beyond Aalst, we discover the hills of Brabant. In the distance, one sees the dome of the Brussels law-courts. We will by-pass the capital and proceed, first to Louvain, with its art treasures, and afterwards, across the Haspengouw plains, in the direction of Liège, "cité ardente" on the banks of the Meuse.

The area around Liège is highly industrialized, but once we cross the Meuse, we reach the pleasant valley of the Vesdre, presenting a synthesis of all the features of the Ardennes.

Spa and Verviers are near-by, as are the high plateaus of the Fagne

STÄDTE UND LANDSCHAFTEN

Eine Übersicht wie diese von Belgien ohne kurze Beschreibung der bedeutendsten touristischen Zentren und Landschaften scheint uns unvollständig; denn sowohl der belgische Reisende wie auch der ausländische Besucher, werden zuerst gefesselt durch den Anblick von Städten und Landschaften mit ihren ins Auge fallenden Reizen, ihrer natürlichen Schönheit und ihren geschichtlichen Monumenten.

Dieses touristische Bild vom Belgien - wie man es nennt, seitdem das Reisen alltäglich und volkstümlich geworden ist -, zeigt eine Fülle andauernd wechselnder Bilder. In diesem kleinen Land ist es unmöglich einige Kilometer zurückzulegen ohne eine Stadt oder ein Dorf anzutreffen, wo nicht ein kostbares Kunstwerk aus seiner rühmlichen Vergangenheit aufbewahrt wird. Es ist auch nicht möglich 30 oder 40 km zurückzulegen, ohne dass die Landschaft sich verändern würde, sodass der Reisende, der Belgien durchkreuzt von Oostende (der Hauptstadt der belgischen Küste) bis Verviers (dem Zentrum der Tuchweberei, ungefähr 20 km von der deutschen Grenze) voll Bewunderung den Eindruck erhält, eine wahre Synthese zu erleben von dem was Europa an Schönheit und Mannigfaltigkeit zu bieten hat.

Zuerst die Nordsee mit ihrem feinen Sandstrand, ihren Seebädern und ihren Dünen. Kaum hat man ihr den Rücken zugekehrt, da erscheinen die Polder, eine Aufeinanderfolge von flachem Land und ungezählten Pappelreihen, die der stets herrschende Seewind landwärts gebogen hat. Nach 20 km sind wir in Brügge, dem Venedig des Nordens, der unvergesslichen mittelalterlichen Stadt, wo man tagelang verbleiben könnte; wir setzen jedoch unsere Reise fort und nach 50 km erreichen wir die Vorstädte von Gent, der Schwesternstadt Brügges in der rühmlichen Vergangenheit der Grafschaft Flandern. Inzwischen hat sich die Landschaft ein paarmal verändert : die Ebene ist übergegangen in leicht hügeliges Gelände. Wir haben nun Aalst hinter uns; nach einigen Kilometern erscheinen bereits die brabantischen Höhenrücken. In der Ferne erhebt sich die Kuppel des Justizpalastes von Brüssel. Wir fahren an der Hauptstadt vorbei und setzen unseren Weg fort, erst in Richtung Löwen, mit seinen zahlreichen Kunstschätzen; darauf

Hesbaye en direction de Liège, la Cité Ardente, située aux rives de la Meuse.

Aux abords de Liège, nous sommes en pleine région industrielle, mais à peine la Meuse franchie, nous entrons dans la riante vallée de la Vesdre, véritable synthèse de tout le pittoresque de l'Ardenne belge.

Spa et Verviers sont maintenant tout proches, de même que les hauts plateaux de la Fagne et les immenses espaces boisés de l'Hertogenwald.

A Bruxelles, le voyageur aurait pu prendre la route en direction d'Anvers, de ses richesses monumentales, de son port et de la Campine anversoise. Il aurait également pu bifurquer en direction de Namur, de la vallée mosane, de Dinant et de tous les sites combien réputés de l'Ardenne belge. Il aurait pu prendre la direction de Charleroi ou de Mons, mais quelle qu'ait été la route de son choix, toujours elle l'aurait conduit vers une ou plusieurs villes d'art; vers quelque région pittoresque.

Comme on le voit, bien que petite, la Belgique est une terre de contrastes et d'infinies variétés dans la répartition de ses sites, aussi divers qu'étonnamment proches les uns des autres.

Pour mettre un peu d'esprit de suite dans cette grande variété, l'on a coutume de partager les richesses naturelles et historiques de la Belgique en trois grandes zones : le littoral, les villes d'art et l'Ardenne, bien qu'on puisse y ajouter d'autres régions d'un intérêt tout aussi important, ainsi la Campine anversoise et limbourgeoise, l'Entre-Sambre-et-Meuse, les Ardennes flamandes aux environs de Renaix, et le Westhoek, non loin d'Ypres.

LE LITTORAL

Suivons donc ce compartimentement traditionnel, pour commencer notre tour de Belgique par une rapide visite du littoral. Trois grands centres retiennent ici l'amateur de vacances balnéaires, ce sont Ostende, Blankenberge et Knokke-Albert-Plage-Le Zoute. De ces trois cités, Ostende est la plus centrale. La ville possède un grand port de pêche, une gare maritime où les malles Ostende-Douvres et les trains internationaux font leur jonction, un hippodrome, un Palais des Thermes et un Kursaal, qui compte parmi les plus réputés d'Europe, ainsi qu'un port de yachting.

Blankenberge est par excellence la plage des familles.

---

gens, door de vlakten van Haspengouw, richting Luik, de vurige stede, gelegen aan de oevers van de Maas. Bij het naderen van Luik rijden wij door een nijverheidsgebied, maar eens over de Maas belanden wij in de lieflijke vallei van de Vesder, die een echte synthese vormt van wat de Belgische Ardennen aan schilderachtigheid te bieden hebben.

Spa en Verviers zijn nu niet ver meer af, evenmin als de vlakten van de Hoge Venen, en de onmetelijke bossen van het Hertogenwoud.

Te Brussel had de reiziger ook de weg kunnen nemen naar Antwerpen, de stad met haar monumentale rijkdommen, haar haven, en naar de Antwerpse Kempen. Hij had ook de andere richting kunnen kiezen naar Namen, de vallei van de Maas, Dinant en vele zo gunstig bekende steden van de Ardennen. Nog andere wegen lagen voor hem open, namelijk naar Charleroi of naar Bergen, maar in elk geval zou hij terecht zijn gekomen in kunststeden of in een schilderachtige streek.

Het blijkt dus dat België, hoewel klein van oppervlakte, een land van contrasten is en een grote verscheidenheid vertoont in de snel wisselende en karakteristieke landschappen.

Met het doel orde te scheppen in deze ruime verscheidenheid, groepeert men de toeristische rijkdommen van België in drie grote zones : de kust, de kunststeden en de Ardennen, hoewel men daarbij toeristisch even belangrijke streken als de Antwerpse en de Limburgse Kempen, Tussen-Samber-en-Maas en de Westhoek zou kunnen voegen.

DE KUST

Laten wij deze traditionele toeristische indeling eerbiedigen, en onze ronde van België beginnen met een vluchtig bezoek aan de kust. Drie grote centra zijn tevens aantrekkingspunten voor de liefhebbers van strandgenot : Oostende, Blankenberge en Knokke - Albert-Plage - Het Zoute. Van deze drie plaatsen neemt Oostende de meest centrale positie in. Deze stad bezit een vissershaven en een haven voor de yachting, een station waar de mailboten Oostende-Dover aansluiting geven op de internationale lijnen, een paardenrenbaan, een thermenpaleis en een Kursaal met Europese faam.

Blankenberge is hoofdzakelijk een

---

and the vast wooded country of the Hertogenwald.

From Brussels, the traveller could have chosen the direction towards Antwerp, with its superb monuments, its harbour, and the Antwerp campine. He also could have branched off towards Namur, the valley of the Meuse, Dinant, and the famous country-side of the Ardennes. Or he could have selected the road towards Charleroi, or Mons. Whatever direction he would have picked out, he would have been making for one, or several, art cities, for a beautiful landscape.

Belgium, however small a country, is an area full of contrasts; the scenery changes constantly, in quick succession.

So as to put some order in all this variety, Belgium is usually divided, according to its natural and historic resources, in three main areas: the coast, the art centres, and the Ardennes. Other regions however are equally important, viz. the Campine in the provinces of Antwerp and Limburg, the area between Meuse and Sambre, the Flemish Ardennes around Ronse, and the Westhoek, near Ieperen.

THE COAST

Let us follow the traditional pattern, and start our tour of Belgium with a short visit to the coast. Three main centres are attacting the seaside holiday-maker: Ostend, Blankenberge, and Knokke-Albert Plage-Het Zoute. The most centrally located of the three is Ostend. It has a large fishing harbour, a maritime station insuring the junction between the Ostend-Dover mailboats and transcontinental trains, a hippodrome, a Thermal Palace, a Kursaal—one of the best known in Europe—and yachting facilities.

Blankenberge is, first and foremost, a sea-side resort for families.

Knokke-Albert Plage-Het Zoute

---

durch die Haspengouw-Ebene in Richtung Lüttich (der feurigen Stadt) an der Maas. Uns Lüttich nähernd, fahren wir durch ein Industriegebiet, doch die Maas überquerend, kommen wir in das liebliche Tal der Vesdre. Hier finden wir alles beieinander, was die belgischen Ardennen Schönes zu bieten haben.

Spa und Verviers sind nun nicht mehr fern, ebenso die Hochebene des Hohen Venn und der ausgedehnte Herzogenwald.

In Brüssel hätte der Reisende auch den Weg nach Antwerpen einschlagen können, (Antwerpen mit seinem Monumentenreichtum, seinem Hafen) und nach dem Antwerpener Kempenland. Er hätte auch die andere Richtung nach Namur und dem Maastal wählen können, nach Dinant und den so bekannten Orten der Ardennen. Noch andere Wege lagen vor ihm offen, nämlich nach Charleroi oder nach Mons. In jedem Fall wäre er zurechtgekommen in Kunststädten oder in einer malerischen Landschaft.

So zeigt sich deutlich, dass Belgien, obwohl klein an Oberfläche, reich an Konstrasten und Sehenswürdigkeiten ist.

Mit dem Ziel Ordnung zu schaffen in dieser grossen Verschiedenheit gruppiert man den touristischen Reichtum Belgiens in drei grosse Zonen : die Küste, die Kunststädte und die Ardennen, obwohl damit touristisch ebenso schöne Gegenden wie die Antwerpener und Limburger Kempen, das Gebiet »Entre Sambre-et-Meuse« und die Westecke übergangen werden.

DIE KÜSTE

Beachten wir diese traditionelle touristische Einteilung und beginnen unsere Tour durch Belgien mit einem flüchtigen Besuch der Küste. Drei grosse Zentren sind die Anziehungspunkte für die Liebhaber des Strandlebens : Oostende, Blankenberge, Knokke - Albert Plage - Het Zoute. Von diesen Orten nimmt Oostende die zentrale Position ein. Diese Stadt besitzt einen Fischerei- und Jachthafen, eine Station, wo die Maildampfer Oostende-Dover mit den internationalen Zügen anschliessen, eine Pferderennbahn, einen Thermenpalast und einen in Europa allgemein bekannten Kursaal.

Blankenberge ist hauptsächlich Familienbad, während Knokke -

Quant à Knokke-Albert Plage-Le Zoute, c'est la grande plage aristocratique et élégante du littoral belge, mais n'oublions ni Heist ni Duinbergen.

Depuis le début de ce siècle, grâce à l'initiative du roi Léopold II, d'ailleurs surnommé le Roi bâtisseur, Bruges se trouve à nouveau réuni à la mer par la construction, entre Knokke et Blankenberge, de son avant-port de Zeebrugge, dont le môle de 2.487 m a permis l'aménagement, en pleine mer, d'une rade de 150 ha de superficie.

Entre Blankenberge et Ostende, il y a les plages de Wenduine, Le Coq et Bredene. Entre Ostende et la frontière française (quelque 30 km à vol d'oiseau) se situent dix autres cités balnéaires toutes soudées plus ou moins les unes aux autres. Elles sont dans l'ordre : Mariakerke, Raversijde, Middelkerke, Westende, Lombardsijde - Bains, Nieuport - Bains, Oostduinkerke, Koksyde, Sint-Idesbald et La Panne.

Parmi les ressources touristiques des plages belges, il convient de citer les excursions vers les villes d'art de l'hinterland de même que vers les souvenirs et les champs de bataille de l'Yser de la guerre 1914-1918.

familiebadplaats, terwijl Knokke - Albert-Strand - Het Zoute het aristocratische en elegante strand van de Belgische kust is.

Sedert het begin van deze eeuw staat Brugge, op initiatief van Koning Leopold II, die trouwens zijn bijnaam van Koning-Bouwer verdiend heeft, opnieuw in verbinding met de zee, ingevolge de aanleg tussen Knokke en Blankenberge, van de voorhaven Zeebrugge. Deze laatste bezit een pier van 2.487 m lengte, die in zee een rede van 150 ha omsluit.

Tussen Zeebrugge en Knokke vermelden we de badplaatsen Heist en Duinbergen.

Tussen Blankenberge en Oostende liggen de stranden van Wenduine, Den Haan en Bredene. Tussen Oostende en de Franse grens (ongeveer 30 km in vogelvlucht) liggen nog een tiental andere badplaatsen, die omzeggens aan elkaar grenzen. Het zijn : Mariakerke, Raversijde, Middelkerke, Westende, Lombardsijde-Bad, Nieuwpoort-Bad, Oostduinkerke, Koksyde, Sint-Idesbald en De Panne.

Tot de toeristische mogelijkheden van de Belgische badplaatsen behoren de uitstapjes naar de kunststeden van het hinterland, naar de gedenktekens en slagvelden van de IJzer, uit de oorlog 1914-1918.

is Belgium's elegant, aristocratic sea-side resort. One should also mention, however, Heist and Duinbergen.

Since the beginning of the century, and thanks to the drive of King Leopold II—also called the Builder-King—Brugge again is linked to the sea, through Zeebrugge's outer harbour—between Knokke and Blankenberge—; a 2,487 m long pier has resulted in the creation of a roadstead of 150 ha in open sea.

Between Blankenberge and Ostend, there are beaches at Wenduine, De Haan, and Bredene. From Ostend to the French border—some 20 miles as the crow flies—there are another ten sea-side resorts, more or less welded to each other. They are, in succession, Mariakerke, Raversijde, Middelkerke, Westende, Lombardsijde-Bad, Nieuwpoort-Bad, Oostduinkerke, Koksyde, St.-Idesbald and De Pànne.

Tourist features of the Belgian coast include possible trips to the art cities in the hinterland and to the landmarks on the Yzer battlefield, in the 1914-1918 war.

Albert Strand - Het Zoute der aristokratische und elegante Strand der belgischen Küste ist.

Seit Beginn dieses Jahrhunderts steht Brügge, durch Initiative König Leopolds II., der übrigens seinen Beinamen »König-Bauherr« verdient hat, aufs neue in Verbindung mit der See, durch das Anlegen des Vorhafens Zeebrügge (zwischen Knokke und Blankenberge), wo eine Mole von 2.487 m Länge in die See gebaut ist, die eine Reede von 150 ha umschliesst.

Zwischen Zeebrügge und Knokke liegen noch die Badeorte Heist und Duinbergen. Die Strände von Wenduine, Den Haan und Bredene befinden sich zwischen Blankenberge und Oostende.

Zwischen Oostende und der französischen Grenze liegen noch zehn andere Badeorte, die jetzt ineinander übergehen : Mariakerke, Raversijde, Middelkerke, Westende, Lombardsijde - Bad, Nieuwpoort - Bad, Oostduinkerke, Koksyde, Sint-Idesbald und De Panne.

Zu den touristischen Möglichkeiten der belgischen Seebäder gehören die Ausflüge zu den Kunststädten im Hinterland und zu den Gedenkstätten und Schlachtfeldern 1914-1918.

L'ARDENNE

Pour ceux qui préfèrent aux larges horizons marins une contrée vallonnée et pittoresque, couverte d'immenses forêts et sillonnée de nombreuses et riantes rivières, la Belgique offre les beautés naturelles de l'Ardenne.

Prenons Namur comme point de départ et remontons la vallée de la Haute-Meuse, en direction de la frontière française. Tantôt sur la rive gauche, tantôt sur la rive droite, nous rencontrerons Jambes, Wépion Profondeville, Lustin, Rivière, Godinne, Annevoie, Yvoir, Anhée, Houx, Bouvignes, Dinant, Anseremme, Freyr, Waulsort, Hermeton et Heer-Agimont.

A Anseremme l'on peut remonter le cours de la Lesse en direction de Rochefort et de Han, dont les grottes sont de réputation mondiale.

Au départ d'Anseremme, également, l'on peut s'aventurer en direction de Beauraing et de là vers la vallée de la Semois aux centres touristiques d'un charme inégalé. La citadelle de Bouillon nous y sera une halte pleine de souvenirs historiques. Plus loin encore c'est la Gaume.

DE ARDENNEN

Voor hen die boven de ruime zeehorizonten een schilderachtige en gegolfde streek verkiezen, bedekt met onmetelijke wouden en doorkruist met talrijke schilderachtige riviertjes, biedt België het natuurschoon van de Ardennen.

Wij nemen Namen als uitgangspunt en richten onze schreden stroomopwaarts langs de vallei van de Opper-Maas naar de Franse grens. Nu eens op de linker- en dan weer op de rechteroever, treffen wij verschillende bekende plaatsen aan: Jambes, Wépion, Profondeville, Lustin, Rivière, Godinne, Annevoie, Yvoir, Anhée, Houx, Bouvignes, Dinant, Anseremme, Freyr, Waulsort, Hermeton en Heer-Agimont.

Van Anseremme uit kan men de loop van de Lesse volgen in de richting van Rochefort en Han, waar men de wereldberoemde grotten kan bezichtigen.

Van Anseremme kan men eveneens de richting van Beauraing inslaan om de vallei van de Semois te bereiken, met haar toeristische centra van een ongeëvenaarde schoonheid. De citadel van Bouillon vormt op onze weg een rustpunt met tal

THE ARDENNES

For those who prefer an undulating, picturesque country-side, with great forests and many charming rivers —rather than the vast expanse and the sea—Belgium offers the resources of the Ardennes.

Starting at Namur, we can go up the Upper Meuse valley, in the direction of the French border. On either side of the banks, we pass Jambes, Wépion, Profondeville, Lustin, Rivière, Godinne, Annevoie, Yvoir, Anhée, Houx, Bouvignes, Dinant, Anseremme, Freyr, Waulsort, Hermeton and Heer-Agimont. At Anseremme, one can go up the valley of the Lesse, towards Rochefort and Han, with their world-famous grottoes.

Also starting from Anseremme, one can wander off in the direction of Beauraing, and, further on, towards the valley of the Semois, with its superb beauty-spots. Bouillon's citadel evokes many historic events. Further on, one reaches the Gaume country.

We push on, to Arlon, with its historic museum, full of Roman antiques.

DIE ARDENNEN

Wer eine malerische, bergige Gegend schöner und abwechlungsreicher findet als den flachen weiten Seehorizont, dem bietet Belgien mit der reichen Natur seiner Ardennen, mit ausgedehnten Wäldern, durchkreuzt von malerischen Flüsschen das Richtige.

Wir nehmen Namur als Ausgangspunkt und richten unsere Schritte stromaufwärts längs des Obermaastals in Richtung der französischen Grenze. Mal auf dem linken, mal auf dem rechten Ufer, treffen wir verschiedene bekannte Orte an : Jambes, Wépion, Profondeville, Lustin, Rivière, Godinne, Annevoie, Yvoir, Anhée, Houx, Bouvignes, Dinant, Anseremme, Freyr, Waulsort, Hermeton und Heer-Agimont.

Von Anseremme aus folgen wir dem Lauf der Lesse in Richtung Rochefort und Han, wo man die weltberühmten Tropfsteinhöhlen besichtigen kann. Man kann auch von Anseremme die Richtung nach Beauraing einschlagen, um das Semoistal zu erreichen, das reich ist an touristischen Sehenswürdigkeiten. Die Zitadelle von Bouillon bietet uns eine Fülle geschichtlicher

Notre route se poursuivra en direction d'Arlon dont le musée archéologique regorge d'antiquités romaines.

Le long de la frontière grand-ducale, nous nous dirigerons vers Bastogne, la cité devenue glorieuse dans les derniers mois de la deuxième guerre mondiale par l'héroïque résistance qu'y opposa l'armée américaine à la ruée de l'offensive Von Rundstedt. En commémoration de ce haut fait d'armes se dresse actuellement à Bastogne un monument grandiose à la mémoire des soldats américains qui y moururent pour le triomphe d'une juste cause.

Un saut de quelques kilomètres et nous pénétrons dans la vallée de l'Ourthe. Voici déjà Houffalize et, descendant le cours occidental de la rivière, nous nous dirigerons vers La Roche, un des centres touristiques les plus connus de l'Ardenne belge. La ville est dominée par les ruines d'un vieux château fort.

Passant par Rendeux, Hotton et Melreux, voici que nous atteignons Durbuy, la plus petite ville de la Belgique avec à peine 300 habitants. Plus loin ce sont Barvaux, Bomal, Logne, Sy et Hamoir. Non loin du confluent de l'Ourthe et de l'Amblève, voici Comblain-au-Pont. Poursuivons notre route en direction de Liège, en passant par Esneux et Tilff. Si nous remontons le cours sinueux de l'Amblève, nous rencontrerons d'abord Aywaille et ensuite Remouchamps avec des grottes moins importantes, mais non moins belles que celles de Han. Plus loin, ce sont les impressionnants fonds de Quarreux, la cascade de Coo et les vastes horizons de la Fagne, justement admirés des amis de la nature.

Rejoignons à présent Malmédy et Eupen avec son immense barrage auquel les barrages de la Warche et de la Gileppe font concurrence en matière de pittoresque.

Et nous voici à Verviers, belle et grande ville industrielle de quelque 42.000 habitants, point de départ d'excursions vers le pays de Herve et de ses magnifiques vergers et pâturages. En quelques kilomètres, l'on rejoindra Spa, une des plus célèbres et des plus vieilles villes d'eau du continent.

Par la riante vallée de la Vesdre, nous rejoindrons la Meuse à Liège, en passant par Chaudfontaine dont le casino moderne est plein d'attraits.

En poursuivant notre périple ar-

van historische herinneringen. Verderop betreden wij het gebied van de Gaume.

Onze weg loopt nu verder naar Aarlen, de hoofdplaats van Luxemburg, waar het archeologisch museum talrijke Romeinse antiquiteiten bezit. Langs de grens van het Groothertogdom slaan wij de weg in naar Bastenaken, de stad die zoveel roem verwierf bij het einde van de tweede wereldoorlog, door de heldhaftige weerstand van het Amerikaanse leger tegen het von Rundstedt-offensief. Ter herdenking van dit wapenfeit is te Bastenaken een grandioos gedenkteken opgericht, gewijd aan de nagedachtenis van de Amerikaanse soldaten, die er sneuvelden voor de rechtvaardige zaak.

Enkele kilometers verder bereiken wij, via Houffalize, de vallei van de Ourthe. De westelijke loop van de rivier volgend, landen wij te La Roche, een der meest bekende toeristische centra van de Belgische Ardennen. Deze stad wordt beheerst door de puinen van een oud versterkt kasteel.

Via Rendeux, Hotton en Melreux bereiken wij Durbuy, het kleinste stadje van België, dat ternauwernood 300 inwoners telt, en verder nog, Barvaux, Bomal, Logne, Sy en Hamoir. Niet ver van het samenvloeien van de Ourthe en de Amblève ligt Comblain-au-Pont. Wij zetten onze weg voort in de richting van Luik, via Esneux en Tilff. Wanneer wij de kronkelige loop van de Amblève volgen, treffen wij eerst Aywaille en vervolgens Remouchamps met zijn grotten die wel minder belangrijk, maar daarom niet minder schoon zijn dan die van Han. Verder bereiken wij de indrukwekkende 'Fonds de Quarreux', de waterval van Coo en de ruime horizonten van de Hoge Venen, die terecht de bewondering wekken van de liefhebbers van natuurschoon.

Vandaar gaat de tocht naar Malmédy en Eupen met zijn reusachtige stuw, die in schilderachtigheid niet moet onderdoen voor die van de Warche en van de Gileppe.

Zo bereiken we Verviers, een grote en schone industriestad met ongeveer 42.000 inwoners, die het uitgangspunt voor uitstapjes naar het land van Herve, met zijn mooie boomgaarden en weilanden. Enkele kilometers verder ligt Spa, een van de beroemdste en oudste kuuroorden van het vasteland. Via het lieflijke dal van de Vesder bereiken wij opnieuw de Maas te Luik, over Chaudfontaine, bekend om zijn modern en aantrekkelijk Casino.

Wij zetten onze tocht door de Ardennen voort langs de Maas, in

On the road running along the border of the Grand-Duchy, we reach Bastogne, the town that is world-famous as a centre of American troups' resistance to the von Rundstedt attack, in the last months of World War II. A magnificent monument has been erected at Bastogne, to commemorate the supreme sacrifice of American soldiers.

A few miles further, we enter the valley of the Ourthe, reaching Houffalize, and, further on, along the Western course of the river, La Roche, one of the best-known tourist resorts of the Ardennes. The ruins of an old fortified castle overlook the town.

Through Rendeux, Hotton and Melreux, we reach Durbuy, Belgium's smallest city, with its mere 300 inhabitants. Further on, we pass through Barvaux, Bomal, Logne, Sy and Hamoir. Comblain-au-Pont is near the junction of the Ourthe and Amblève rivers. As we proceed further towards Liège, we pass Esneux and Tilff. Upwards the meandering course of the Amblève, we reach, first Aywaille, and subsequently Remouchamps, with its caves that are smaller than, but as beautiful as, those at Han. Further on, we see the impressive estates at Quarreux, the waterfall at Coo and the broad horizons of the Fagne country, greatly admired by lovers of the country-side.

We now arrive at Malmedy and Eupen, with its huge dam, that competes, in elegance and beauty, with those of the Warche and the Gileppe.

We are reaching Verviers, a large, beautiful industrial city (42,000 inhabitants), from where one can make excursions to the Herve country, with its superb orchards and pastures. A few miles further, there is Spa, one of the oldest and most famous watering resorts on the continent.

Through the pleasant valley of the Vesdre, we reach the Meuse at Liège, passing through Chaudfontaine, with its attractive, modern casino.

Continuing our tour of the Ardennes with a walk along the Meuse towards Huy and Namur, we cross the industrial area around the big city, soon to re-discover the country-side. Huy is a charming holiday resort, and its gothic collegiate church has many works of art. The

Erinnerungen, und weiter weg betreten wir die naturwüchsige Gegend der Gaume.

Dann setzen wir unseren Weg fort nach Arlon, der Hauptstadt der Provinz Luxemburg, wo das archeologische Museum zahlreiche römische Altertümer bewahrt. Längs der Grenze des Grossherzogtums schlagen wir den Weg nach Bastogne ein, das gegen Ende des zweiten Weltkrieges berühmt wurde durch den heldhaften Widerstand der amerikanischen Armee gegen die Rundstedt-Offensive. Zum Andenken an diese Waffentat ist in Bastogne ein grosses Denkmal aufgerichtet, das dem Andenken der gefallenen amerikanischen Soldaten gewidmet ist. Mit einem Sprung von einigen Kilometern erreichen wir über Houffalize das Ourthetal. Wenn wir der Westourthe folgen, kommen wir nach La Roche, einen der bekanntesten Touristenorte der belgischen Ardennen. Die Stadt wird beherrscht durch die Ruinen eines alten Schlosses.

Über Rendeux, Hotton und Melreux gelangen wir nach Durbuy, dem kleinsten Städtchen Belgiens, welches kaum 300 Einwohner zählt. Weiter kommen wir nach Barvaux, Bomal, Sy und Hamoir. Nicht weit vom Zusammenfluss von Ourthe und Amblève liegt Comblain-au-Pont. Wir setzen unseren Weg fort in Richtung Lüttich, über Esneux und Tielff. Wenn wir dem gewundenen Lauf der Amblève folgen, kommen wir erst nach Aywaille und dann nach Remouchamps mit den Höhlen, die wohl weniger gross, aber darum nicht weniger schön als die von Han sind.

Weiterweg erreichen wir die imposante »Fonds de Quarreux«, den Wasserfall von Coo und die weiten Horizonte des Hohen Venn, die zu Recht die Bewunderung des Naturliebhabers wecken. Von dort geht die Fahrt nach Malmédy und Eupen mit seinem riesigen Staudamm, der ebenso wie der von der Warche und der Gileppe einen unvergesslichen Eindruck hinterlässt.

So erreichen wir Verviers, eine grosse und schöne Industriestadt mit ca 42.000 Einwohnern, dem Ausgangspunkt von Ausflügen zum Lande von Herve mit seinen schönen Baumgärten und Weiden.

Einige Kilometer weiter liegt Spa, einer der berühmtesten und ältesten Kurorte des Kontinents. Durch das liebliche Vesdretal erreichen wir aufs Neue die Maas zu Lüttich, nachdem wir Chaudfontaine, bekannt durch sein modernes, anziehendes Kasino, passiert haben.

dennais par une promenade le long de la Meuse en direction de Huy et Namur, nous dépasserons la région industrielle de la grande cité mosane, avant que la nature ne reprenne ses droits. A Huy, nous nous retrouvons dans un centre de villégiature, dont la collégiale gothique recèle bien des richesses artistiques. Du haut de la citadelle, le panorama est prestigieux.

Avant d'arriver à Namur nous ferons encore une halte pieuse au rocher de Marche-les-Dames, où le roi Albert trouva, le 17 février 1934, une mort tragique.

A Namur, la promenade de la citadelle s'impose, car le panorama sur la vallée de la Meuse y est de toute beauté. Recommandons également une halte au casino de la ville. A présent mettons-nous en route vers l'Entre-Sambre-et-Meuse où plus d'un bourg, pittoresquement blotti parmi les prés et les bois, pourra retenir le touriste épris de calme et de promenades solitaires.

de richting van Hoei en Namen, doorkruisen het grote nijverheidsgebied van de oude Maasstad, om daarna weer te genieten van de volle natuur. Hoei is een villegiatuurcentrum met een gotische kathedraal vol kunstschatten. Van op de Citadel geniet men van een enig panorama.

Alvorens Namen te bereiken houden wij even halt bij de rots te Marche-les-Dames, waar Koning Albert op 17 februari 1934 tragisch aan zijn einde kwam.

Te Namen moet men beslist de wandeling naar de Citadel maken, om van daar uit de schoonheid van het panorama van de Maasvallei te kunnen bewonderen. Wij kunnen ook gerust een bezoek aan het Casino van de stad aanbevelen, waarna wij ons weer op weg begeven naar Tussen-Samber-en-Maas, waar meer dan één stadje, schilderachtig geborgen tussen weiden en bossen, de aandacht trekt van de toerist die houdt van rust en eenzame wandelingen.

view, from the citadel, is breathtaking.

Before reaching Namur, we will stop at the rock at Marche-les-Dames, where, on February 17, 1934, King Albert found a tragic death.

In Namur, one should walk up to the citadel, for the view there of the Meuse valley is superb. A stop at the city's casino is also a worthwhile experience. And we move on to the area between Meuse and Sambre, where many a hamlet among meadows and near-by woods will attract the tourist in search of peace and solitary walks.

Am Ufer der Maas setzen wir unseren Weg in Richtung Namur fort, durchqueren das grosse Industriegebiet der alten Maasstadt, um danach wieder die weite Natur zu geniessen. In Huy, bekanntem Ferienort, bewundern wir die gotische Kathedrale, die viele Kunstschätze besitzt. Von der Zitadelle geniesst man ein wunderbares Panorama. Bevor wir Namur erreichen, halten wir eben beim Felsen von Marche-les-Dames, berühmt durch das tödliche Unglück Albert I.

In Namur muss man unbedingt einen Spaziergang zur Zitadelle machen, um von dort die einzigartige Aussicht über das Maastal zu bewundern. Wir empfehlen auch den Besuch des Kasinos, wonach wir uns wieder auf den Weg machen nach dem Gebiet »Entre-Sambre-et-Meuse«, wo mehr als ein Städtchen malerisch versteckt zwischen Wald und Weiden, die Andacht der Reisenden fesseln wird, vor allem derer die Ruhe und einsame Spaziergänge lieben.

LES AUTRES RÉGIONS

Bien d'autres coins de l'Ardenne seraient encore à mentionner, car tous recèlent des richesses naturelles qui peuvent charmer et retenir les touristes épris des beautés d'un paysage sans cesse changeant.

Il nous faudrait également pouvoir conduire les amants de la nature vers d'autres régions du pays tout aussi pittoresques, mais comment citer et décrire toutes ces contrées si différentes les unes des autres, bien que toutes soient si proches les unes des autres et distantes de la capitale de quelques 100 km au maximum. Citons toutefois la Campine avec ses dunes, ses marais et ses bois de sapin, les polders aux horizons lointains aux abords de l'Escaut maritime; les Ardennes flamandes, aux environs de Renaix, et les monts de Flandres, au sud d'Ypres; les châteaux historiques du Tournaisis, dont le fameux château des princes de Ligne, à Beloeil.
Mais n'oublions point le Brabant wallon dont le grand centre d'attraction est toujours le champ de bataille de Waterloo.

DE ANDERE STREKEN

Tal van andere hoekjes van de Ardennen zouden moeten vermeld worden. Ze bezitten immers natuurlijke rijkdommen die de toerist, die houdt van afwisseling, kunnen bekoren en aantrekken.

Wij zouden de natuurliefhebbers naar andere streken van het land kunnen voeren die even schilderachtig zijn, maar het is niet mogelijk al die streken, die aan elkaar grenzen en toch grondig verschillen en ten hoogste 100 km van de hoofdstad zijn verwijderd, op te sommen en te beschrijven. Alleen vermelden wij hier de Kempen met haar duinen, moerassen en dennebossen; de Polders, met de verre horizonten in de buurt van de Zeeschelde; de Vlaamse Ardennen in de buurt van Ronse, en de Vlaamse heuvelen ten zuiden van Ieper; de historische kastelen van het Doornikse waaronder het befaamde kasteel van de prinsen de Ligne te Beloeil.

Ten slotte denken we aan Waals-Brabant, waarvan het grote aantrekkingspunt het slagveld van Waterloo is.

THE OTHER REGIONS

Many other places in the Ardennes would deserve to be mentioned. All of them hold natural resources, attracting tourists who like a constant change in scenery.

Lovers of nature also should be led towards other areas of the country, but it is impossible to quote and describe them all, in their unique diversity, so close to each other, and located at a maximum distance of some 60 miles from the capital. We want to mention the Campine, with its dunes, its moors, and forests of pines; the Flemish Ardennes, in the Ronse area, and the Flanders mountains, South of Ieperen; the historic castles in the Tournai country, i.a. the well-known castle of Beloeil, belonging to the princes de Ligne.

We should not forget the Walloon part of Brabant, with the battlefield of Waterloo as a permanent pole of attraction.

DIE ANDEREN GEGENDEN

Zahllose andere Winkel der Ardennen müssten erwähnt werden; sie alle besitzen Naturschönheiten die den Touristen, besonders den, der die Abwechslung liebt, bezaubern und anziehen würden. Wir müssten den Naturliebhaber noch zu anderen Gegenden führen, die ebenso malerisch sind; aber es ist nicht möglich alle diese Landschaften aufzuzählen, die aneinander grenzen und doch so verschieden und höchstens 100 km von der Hauptstadt entfernt sind. Wir verweisen hier allein auf die Kempen mit seinen Dünen, Sümpfen und Tannenwäldern; die Polder mit den weiten Horizonten in der Gegend der Seeschelde; die flämischen Ardennen in der Umgebung von Ronse, und die flämischen Hügel südlich von Ieper, die historischen Schlösser um Tournai, darunter das berühmte Schloss der Fürsten de Ligne zu Beloeil.

Zum Schluss denken wir an wallonisch Brabant, dessen grosser Anziehungspunkt das Schlachtfeld von Waterloo ist.

LES VILLES D'ART

A présent que nous avons rendu un juste tribu aux beautés naturelles de la Belgique, nous nous permettrons une rapide évocation des richesses artistiques que recèlent entre

DE KUNSTSTEDEN

Nu wij een eresaluut gebracht hebben aan het natuurschoon van België, willen wij ook in 't kort de kunstschatten vermelden, die de grote kunststeden als Antwerpen, Brugge,

THE CITIES OF THE ART

Now that we have paid tribute to Belgium's natural resources, we want rapidly to evoke the wealth of art treasures in the large cities: Antwerp, Brugge, Brussels, Ghent,

DIE KUNSTSTÄDTE

Nun wir einen Ehrensalut auf die Schönheit der Natur ausgebracht haben, wollen wir kurz die Sehenswürdigkeiten der grossen Kunststädte, Antwerpen, Brügge, Brüssel,

leurs murs les grandes villes d'art que sont Anvers, Bruges, Bruxelles, Gand, Liège, Mons, Namur et Tournai. Mais ici protesteront aussitôt les fervents de villes tout aussi riches en trésors artistiques comme Audenarde, Lierre, Louvain, Malines, Nivelles, pour n'en citer que quelques-unes, aussi les évoquerons nous, également à leur tour.

Brussel, Gent, Luik, Bergen, Namen en Doornik bewaren, op gevaar af het protest uit te lokken van enkele niet minder rijke steden, als Oudenaarde, Lier, Leuven, Mechelen en Nijvel, om er slechts enkele te noemen.

Liège, Mons, Namur and Tournai. Some will rightly claim that other cities also qualify here, such as Oudenaarde, Lier, Leuven, Mechelen, Nivelles. We also will do them justice.

Gent, Lüttich, Mons, Namur und Tournai aufzählen, auf die Gefahr des Protestes der anderen Städte hin, die ebensoviele Sehenswürdigkeiten bergen – wie Oudenaarde, Lier, Löwen, Mechelen und Nivelles, (um nur einige zu nennen, die jedoch später erwähnt werden sollen).

ANVERS

Outre l'incomparable intérêt touristique de son port que l'on peut aisément visiter en bateau, la ville d'Anvers offre à l'admiration du touriste, toute une gerbe de monuments les uns plus remarquables encore que les autres. Il y a tout d'abord la cathédrale Notre-Dame (XIVe-XVIe siècle) avec sa tour haute de 123 m et ses chefs-d'œuvre de Rubens, il y a ensuite l'hôtel de ville en style Renaissance, de même que les églises Saint-Jacques (XVe siècle) avec le tombeau de Rubens, Saint-Augustin (XVIIe siècle), Saint-Charles-Borromée (XVIIe siècle) et Saint-André (XVIe siècle), pour ne citer que les principales. Toutes regorgent d'œuvres d'art. Au chapitre des musées, citons le Musée Royal des Beaux-Arts, le Musée Plantin-Moretus, le Musée Mayer Van den Bergh (un des plus riches petits musées qu'il y ait au monde), la Maison des Bouchers, la Maison des Brasseurs, le Steen, de même que la maison de Rubens, si royalement restituée en sa splendeur d'antan. Le jardin zoologique mérite certes, une mention spéciale car il est non seulement le plus connu que possède la Belgique, mais aussi un des plus riches du monde.

ANTWERPEN

Behalve in de onvergelijkelijke toeristische belangstelling voor haar haven, die per plezierboot kan bezichtigd worden, kan Antwerpen zich verheugen in de bewondering van de toerist voor haar talrijke en merkwaardige monumenten : in de eerste plaats de Onze-Lieve-Vrouwkathedraal (14de-16de eeuw) met haar 123 m hoge toren en haar meesterwerken van Rubens; verder het stadhuis in renaissance-stijl, de Sint-Jacobskerk (15de eeuw) met het graf van Rubens, de Sint-Augustinuskerk (17de eeuw), de kerk van de H. Carolus-Borromeus (17de eeuw) en de Sint-Andrieskerk (16de eeuw), om slechts de voornaamste te noemen. Alle bezitten ze een overvloed aan merkwaardige kunstwerken. Als musea verdienen een bijzondere vermelding : het Koninklijk Museum voor Schone Kunsten, het Plantijn- en Moretus-Museum, het Museum Mayer-Van den Bergh, een van de rijkste kleine musea van België, het Vleeshuis, het Brouwershuis, het Steen en ook het huis van Rubens, dat opnieuw schittert in zijn vroegere koninklijke luister. De Dierentuin verdient een aparte vermelding als grootste in zijn soort in België en tevens als een der merkwaardigste ter wereld.

ANTWERP

Besides the great attraction that the harbour holds for tourists,—who can easily tour it by boat—Antwerp offers a series of striking monuments : the cathedral church, dedicated to Our Lady (14th-16th centuries) with its 123 m high spire and its Rubens master-pieces; the city hall, in Renaissance style, and the churches dedicated to St. James (15th century) with Rubens' tomb, St. Augustine (17th century), St. Charles-Borromeo (17th century), St. Andrew (16th century), to name but a few. All are full of works of art. In the sector of the museums, we should mention the Royal Museum of Fine Arts, the Museum Plantin-Moretus, the Museum Mayer Van den Bergh (one of the world's richest, small-sized museums), the Butchers' House, the Brewers' House, the Steen, and Rubens's residence, magnificently restored in its pristine splendour. The zoological garden deserves a special mark, for it is Belgium's best-known garden of its kind, and one of the best-stocked in the world.

ANTWERPEN

Wenn man Antwerpen sagt, denkt man zuerst an den Hafen, der mit einem Ausflugdampfer besichtigt werden kann. Um die zahlreichen und merkwürdigen Monumente aufzuzählen, beginnen wir erst mit der U.L.Fraukathedrale (14.-16. Jh.) mit ihrem 123 m hohen Turm und den Gemälden von Rubens, dem Renaissancerathaus, der St Jakobkirche (15. Jh.) mit dem Grabe von Rubens, der St Augustinuskirche (17. Jh.), der Kirche des H. Carolus-Borromäus (17. Jh.) und der St Andreaskirche (16. Jh.), um nur die bedeutendsten zu nennen. Alle besitzen eine Fülle bemerkenswerter Kunstwerke. Als Museum verdient das Königl. Museum für Schöne Künste, das Plantijn- und Moretusmuseum, das Museum Mayer - Van den Bergh (eines der reichsten kleinen Museen Belgiens), das Fleischhaus, das Brauershaus, der »Steen« und auch das Haus Rubens, welches aufs Neue in seinem früheren königlichen Glanz schimmert, eine besondere Erwähnung. Auch den Zoologischen Garten dürfen wir nicht vergessen, denn er ist der grösste seiner Art in Belgien und ausserdem der bemerkenswerteste der Welt.

BRUGES

Toute la ville de Bruges n'est qu'un grand musée en plein air avec ses monuments innombrables, ses canaux romantiques et son paisible béguinage. Trois tours dominent la cité : celle du beffroi, au centre des halles (XIIIe-XVe siècles), sur la grand-place, et celles des églises Notre-Dame et Saint-Sauveur (la cathédrale). Sur la place du Bourg s'élèvent plusieurs monuments remarquables : l'hôtel de ville (XIVe siècle), l'Ancien Greffe (XVIe siècle) du Franc de Bruges, le palais de justice (XVIIIe siècle) avec sa belle cheminée, la basilique du Saint-Sang avec sa crypte romane de Saint-Basile et sa chapelle supérieure (XVe siècle) où se trouve conservée

BRUGGE

De gehele stad Brugge met haar ontelbare monumenten, haar romantische reien en haar vreedzaam begijnhof is als het ware een openluchtmuseum. Drie torens beheersen de stad : die van het Belfort, te midden van de Hallen (13de-15de eeuw) op de Grote Markt, die van de Onze-Lieve-Vrouwekerk en die van de Sint-Salvatorskathedraal. Op de Burg verheffen zich verscheidene merkwaardige monumenten : het stadhuis (14de eeuw), de oude griffie (16de eeuw), het gerechtshof (18de eeuw) met de mooie schoorsteen van het Brugse Vrije, de basiliek van het H. Bloed met haar romaanse krocht van de H. Basilius en haar kapel waarin de relikwie

BRUGES

Brugge—with its countless monuments, its romatic canals and quiet beguine convent—is one vast open-air museum. Three towers dominate the city: the belfry, centre of the city hall on the market-place (13th-15th centuries), and those of the Our-Lady, and St. Saviour churches. Several remarkable munuments are grouped around the city hall (14th century), the old record-office (16th century), the Bruges Exemption, law courts (18th century), with its beautiful fireplace, the basilica of the Holy Blood with its romanesque St. Basil crypt and its upper chapel (15th century) where the reliquary of the Holy Blood is kept, and the Provostry (17th century). Among

BRÜGGE

Die ganze Stadt Brügge mit ihren unzähligen Monumenten, ihren romantische Grachten (reien genannt) und ihrem friedlichen Beginenhof ist ein wahres Museum. Drei Türme beherrschen die Stadt : der Bergfried (Belfort) mit den Hallen (13.-15. Jh.) auf dem »Grote Markt«, der der Frauenkirche und der der St. Salvatorkathedrale. Auf dem Burgplatz erheben sich verschiedene bedeutende Monumente : das Rathaus (14. Jh.), die alte »Griffie« (Kanzlei, 14. Jh.), der Gerichtshof (18. Jh.) mit dem schönen Kamin des »Brugse Vrije«, die Basilika des Hl. Blutes mit ihrer romanischen Krypta des H. Basilius und der Kapelle, in der die Reliquie des

la relique du Saint-Sang et enfin la Maison de la Prévôté (XVIIe siècle). Au chapitre des monuments civils, il convient de citer le musée Gruuthuuse, l'hôpital Saint-Jean (avec ses Memlincs), la Poorterslogie ainsi que de nombreuses maisons patriciennes de tous les styles, depuis le style gothique jusqu'au style Louis XVI. Parmi les musées, il convient avant tout de visiter le Musée municipal avec ses incomparables Primitifs flamands : les frères Van Eyck, Roger van der Weyden, Hugo van der Goes, Memlinc, Jérôme Bosch, etc.; le Musée Gruuthuuse ainsi que la maison natale du poète flamand Guido Gezelle.

van het H. Bloed wordt bewaard, ten slotte de Proostdij (17de eeuw). Tot de burgerlijke monumenten behoren het Gruuthuuse-museum, het Sint-Janshospitaal met zijn Memlingmuseum, de Poorterslogie en talrijke patriciërshuizen in alle stijlen, van de gotische tot de Lodewijk XVI-stijl. Van de musea die een bezoek waard zijn vernoemen wij : het Gemeentelijk Museum met zijn belangrijke verzameling Vlaamse Primitieven, waaronder de gebroeders Van Eyck, Rogier van der Weyden, Hugo van der Goes, Memling, Jeroen Bosch, e.a.; het Gruuthuuse-Museum, evenals het geboortehuis van de Vlaamse dichter, Guido Gezelle.

the secular monuments, one should note the Museum Gruuthuuse, St. John's Hospital (with its Memlings), the "Poorterslogie" and several patrician mansions in various styles, from gothic to Louis XVI. Under the museums, priority should be given to the municipal museum, with its outstanding Flemish gothic ("primitive") painters: the Van Eyck brothers, Roger van der Weyden, Hugo van der Goes, Memlinc, Jerome Bosch, etc... Further worth visiting are the Gruuthuuse museum and the house where Guido Gezelle, the Flemish poet, was born.

Hl. Blutes aufbewahrt wird, und zum Schluss die Propstei (17. Jh.). Zu den Bürgerbauten gehören das Gruuthuusemuseum, das St. Jansspital mit seinem Memlingmuseum, die »Poorterslogie« und zahlreiche Patrizierhäuser in verschiedenen Stilen, vom gotischen bis zum Ludwig XVI.-Stil. Unter den Museen, die einen Besuch besonders wert sind, nennen wir das Gemeindemuseum mit seinen unvergleichlichen flämischen Primitiven : Jan van Eyck, Rogier van der Weyden, Hugo van der Goes, Memling, Jeroen Bosch u.a., das Gruuthuuse-Museum, sowie das Geburtshaus des grossen flämischen Dichters Guido Gezelle (19. Jh.).

BRUXELLES

Si la capitale du royaume est riche en monuments de toutes sortes, elle s'orgueillit cependant avant tout de posséder une des plus belles places publiques qu'il y ait au monde : la grand-place, avec son hôtel de ville gothique, sa Maison du Roi en style néo-gothique et ses maisons des Corporations en style baroque tardif, où pointe le style Louis XIV. Tout proche de cette magnificence, le touriste est attiré par une autre attraction, infiniment plus modeste il est vrai, mais de réputation tout aussi universelle, c'est la petite fontaine publique de style baroque communément appelée Manneken-Pis. La cathédrale Saint-Michel (XIVe-XVIe siècle), tout au haut de la butte du Treurenberg, est pleine de majesté, avec ses deux tours massives et ses incomparables vitraux Renaissance.

Depuis peu, un nouveau boulevard conduit le promeneur depuis le Jardin Botanique à l'église de la Chapelle (XIIIe siècle) où se trouve le tombeau de Pierre Breughel l'Ancien. Au passage il admirera la Banque nationale, la gare Air-Terminus de la Sabena, la gare Centrale, le nouveau Mont des Arts et la nouvelle bibliothèque Albertine. Depuis l'église de la Chapelle, le promeneur remontera vers la rue de la Régence, véritable rue monumentale. Au Grand Sablon, voici l'église Notre-Dame des Victoires (XVe siècle), puis le square du Petit Sablon. Au fond de la rue de la Régence, à droite, se dresse le gigantesque palais de justice que surmonte une coupole pleine de majesté. Au coin du Petit Sablon, s'élève le Conservatoire Royal de Musique avec son musée instrumental, un des plus riches du monde. Dans la même rue encore, mais en direction

BRUSSEL

De hoofdstad van België is wel rijk aan tal van monumenten, maar ze is er vooral trots op een van de mooiste openbare pleinen ter wereld te bezitten, namelijk de Grote Markt met haar gotisch stadhuis, haar Broodhuis in neo-gotische stijl en haar laat-barokke gildehuizen, waarin reeds de Lodewijk XIV-stijl doorschemert. In de nabijheid van al deze pracht wordt de toerist aangetrokken tot een andere bezienswaardigheid, die weliswaar bescheidener is, maar die niettemin wereldfaam heeft verkregen : het kleine openbare barokfonteintje, algemeen bekend als Manneken-Pis. Op de heuvel van de Treurenberg, verheft de Sint-Michielskathedraal (14de-16de eeuw) statig haar twee massieve torens. De kerk bezit ook merkwaardige glasramen uit de Renaissancetijd.

Sedert korte tijd voert een nieuwe laan de wandelaar van de Kruidtuin naar de Kapellekerk (13de eeuw), waar zich het graf van Pieter Breughel de Oude bevindt. In het voorbijgaan treft hij de Nationale Bank aan, de Sabena-terminus, het Centraal Station, de nieuwe Albertina-bibliotheek met de eveneens nieuwe Kunstberg. Van de Kapellekerk klimt de wandelaar op naar de Regentiestraat, waar de monumenten elkaar opvolgen. Aan de Grote Zavel verheft zich de kerk van Onze-Lieve-Vrouw-ter-Zege (15de eeuw), vlak tegenover de Kleine Zavel. Aan het eind van de Regentiestraat rijst het reusachtige Justitiepaleis op met zijn statige koepel. Naast de Kleine Zavel staat het Koninklijk Muziekconservatorium, waarvan het instrumentenmuseum een van de rijkste ter wereld is. In dezelfde straat, maar in de richting van het Koningsplein, zien wij links

BRUSSELS

The capital of the Kingdom offers a wealth of monuments of all kinds, and has, moreover, one of the world's most beautiful market-places: the "Grand-Place", with its gothic city hall, its "Maison du Roi" in neo-gothic style, and its Corporation houses in late baroque announcing the Louis XIV style. In the vicinity of all this splendour, the tourist discovers another, far more modest, but equally famous attraction: the small public fountain in baroque style generally called Manneken-Pis. The St. Michael cathedral (14th-16th centuries), on top of the Treurenberg mound, is a majestic building, with its two heavy towers and its superb Renaissance stained glass windows.

In recent years, a new boulevard has been built between the Botanical Garden and the Chapelle Church (13th century) which houses the tomb of Peter Breughel the Elder. In-between, the tourist will see the National Bank, the Sabena Air-Terminal, the central station, the new "Mont des Arts" and the Albertine library. Form the Chapelle church, he will walk towards the rue de la Régence, with its monumental buildings. At the Grand Sablon stands the church dedicated to Notre-Dame des Victoires (15th century), and a few yards further, the square of the Petit Sablon. In the background rises the huge building of the Courts of Justice, with its majestic dome. At one of the street's corners, he will notice the Royal Conservatoire of Music, with its museum of musical instruments, one of the richest in the world. In the same street, but in the direction of the Rue Royale, on the left hand side, there is the façade of the

BRÜSSEL

Die Hauptstadt Belgiens, reich an Monumenten, ist vor allem stolz darauf, einen der schönsten, öffentlichen Plätze der Welt zu besitzen, nämlich den »Grand'Place« mit seinem gotischen Rathaus, dem »Broodhuis« in neugotischem Stil und den spätbarocken Zunfthäusern, bei denen der Ludwig XIV.-Stil bereits durchschimmert. Nach dieser Pracht wird der Tourist angezogen durch eine andere Sehenswürdigkeit, die zwar bescheidener im Ausmass, aber trotsdem weltberühmt ist : der kleine öffentliche Barockbrunnen, algemein bekannt als »Manneken Pis«. Die St. Michaelskathedrale auf dem »Treurenberg« erhebt majestätisch ihre zwei massiven Türme. Sie besitzt bermerkenswerte Renaissanceglasrahmen.

Seit einiger Zeit führt eine neue breite Strasse den Spaziergänger von dem ehemaligen Botanischen Garten zur Kapellenkirche (13. Jh.), wo sich das Grab Pieter Breughels des Alten befindet. Auf dem Wege dorthin kommt man vorbei an der Nationalen Bank, dem Sabenaterminus, am Zentral Bahnhof, der neuen Albertina-Bibliothek auf dem Kunstberg. Von der Kapellenkirche steigt der Spaziergänger auf nach der Rue de la Régence, wo die Monumente aufeinanderfolgen. An dem »Grand Sablon« erhebt sich die Frauenkirche (15. Jh.) direkt gegenüber dem »Petit Sablon«. Am Ende der Rue de la Régenèe liegt der riesengrosse Justizpalast mit seiner gewaltigen Kuppel. Neben dem »Petit Sablon« steht das Königliche Musikkonservatorium, dessen Instrumentenmuseum eines der reichsten der Welt ist. In derselben Strasse, doch in Richtung des Königsplatzes, sehen wir links die

de la place Royale, voici à gauche la façade du Musée Royal des Beaux-Arts, La place Royale, elle, est un ensemble néo-classique ou plutôt Louis XVI de la fin du XVIIIe siècle, comparable pour son ordonnance à certaines places françaises. Elle est dominée par la façade de l'église Saint-Jacques sur Coudenberg et en son centre se trouve le monument Godefroid de Bouillon. Sous un portique, l'on débouche sur la paisible place du Musée, avec l'ancienne Bibliothèque Royale et les vestiges du Musée d'Art Moderne, ancien palais du duc Charles de Lorraine. De la place Royale, l'on passe à la place des Palais. Ici nous avons les verdures du parc de Bruxelles, l'imposant palais Royal du début de ce siècle, ainsi que la façade néo-classique du Palais des Académies. La rue de la Loi possède le bel ensemble Louis XVI que forment le palais de la Nation ainsi que plusieurs hôtels ministériels. La perspective est fermée au loin par l'arc de triomphe du Cinquantenaire (1905). Dans la rue Royale, voici la colonne du Congrès (1850-1859) et la tombe du Soldat Inconnu. Plus loin, devant le Jardin Botanique, nous découvrons d'une part l'église Sainte-Marie et de l'autre la basilique nationale du Sacré-Cœur, à Koekelberg.

Notre périple du Bruxelles monumental et touristique se terminera par une promenade le long des boulevards du centre. Nous rencontrerons ainsi au passage la place de Brouckère, avec son monument Anspach, et la Bourse (1875). Depuis quelque dix ans Bruxelles s'est également enrichi de plusieurs buildings-gratte-ciel ainsi que d'un Atomium haut de 110 m et aux formes originales qui rappellent celles de l'atome.

Bruxelles est riche en musées de tous genres : beaux-arts, archéologie musique, ethnographie et sciences naturelles. Leurs collections sont en tout comparables à celles des plus grands musées du monde.

Méritent une mention spéciale, dans la banlieue bruxelloise, le Musée de l'Afrique Centrale, à Tervueren, et la Maison d'Érasme, à Anderlecht.

Dans le parc de Laeken, attirons l'attention sur la résidence de la famille royale, sur celle du prince de Liège, ainsi que sur le Pavillon Chinois, la Tour Japonaise et les serres royales.

de voorgevel van het Koninklijk Museum voor Schone Kunsten. Het hierbij aansluitende Koningsplein is een neo-klassiek geheel in typische Lodewijk XVI-stijl en dagtekent uit het eind van de 18de eeuw. In zijn aanleg kan het vergeleken worden met sommige Franse openbare pleinen. Het wordt beheerst door de voorgevel van de kerk van Sint-Jacob-op-de-Koudenberg en midden op het plein staat het monument opgericht ter nagedachtenis van Godfried van Bouillon. Langs een portiek belandt men op het Museumplein met de gewezen Koninklijke Bibliotheek en het voormalige Museum voor Moderne Kunst, voorheen het paleis van hertog Karel van Lorreinen. Van het Koningsplein is het maar één stap naar het Paleizenplein, dat gelegen is tussen het groene stadspark van Brussel, het indrukwekkende Koninklijk Paleis uit het begin dezer eeuw en de neo-klassieke voorgevel van het Paleis der Academiën. In de Wetstraat bevinden zich het Parlementsgebouw en verscheidene ministeriële ambtsgebouwen, die een sierlijk geheel vormen in Lodewijk XVI-stijl. In de verte wordt de horizont gesloten door de triomfboog van het Jubelpark (1905). Wanneer wij de Koningsstraat afdalen bereiken wij eerst de Congreskolom (1850-59) met het Graf van de Onbekende Soldaat, verder, voorbij de Kruidtuin, de Sint-Mariakerk, en links in de verte de Nationale Basiliek van het Heilig Hart, te Koekelberg.

Onze speurtocht naar de monumenten en toeristische bezienswaardigheden van Brussel besluiten wij met een wandeling langs de middenlanen. Op het de Brouckèreplein treffen wij aldus het Anspachgedenkteken, en iets verder het Beursgebouw (1875).

Brussel is rijk aan musea van alle aard, gewijd aan de schone kunsten, de archeologie, de muziek, de etnografie en de natuurhistorie.

In de Brusselse randgemeenten dienen vermeld te worden : het Museum voor Centraal Afrika te Tervuren en het Erasmushuis te Anderlecht, terwijl we aan de andere kant van de stad, te Laken, de aandacht vestigen op de Residentie van de koninklijke familie, op deze van de prinsen van Luik, het Chinese paviljoen, de Japanse toren, de koninklijke broeikassen en het Atomium.

Royal Museum of Fine Arts. The place Royale is a neo-classical, or rather late 18th century Louis XVI arrangement, recalling some public places in France. The square is commanded by the façade of the St. Jacques sur Coudenberg church, and in the middle rises the statue of Godefroid de Bouillon. Through a portico, one reaches the quiet Place du Musée, with the old Royal Library and the remains of the Museum of Modern Art,—the former palace of the duke Charles de Lorraine. From the place Royale, one walks on to the place des Palais, with the charming layout of the Parc de Bruxelles, the imposing Royal Palace built in the early years of the century, and the neo-classical front of the Palais des Académies. In the rue de la Loi, there is the fine Louis XVI set of buildings housing the Belgian Parliament, together with some ministerial residences. The perspective is closed, in the distance, by the triumphal arch of the Cinquantenaire (1905). In the rue Royale, one notices the colonne du Congrès (1850-1859), and the tomb of the Unknown Warrior. Further on, in front of the Botanical Garden, we see the Sainte Marie church on one side and, on the other, the national basilica of the Sacré-Cœur, at Koekelberg.

Our walk through Brussels will end with a stroll along the central boulevards. This will take us past the place de Brouckère, with its monument to Anspach, and the Stock Exchange. In the last ten years, Brussels also has seen the construction of a number of skyscrapers, and of a 110 m high Atomium, which reproduces the structure of an atom.

Brussels has a wealth of museums of all kinds: fine arts, archeology, music, ethnography, and natural sciences. Their respective collections are as worth-while as those of the world's finest museums.

A special mention should be made, in the Brussels suburbs, of the Museum of Central Africa, at Tervuren, and the Erasmus House, at Anderlecht.

In the parc at Laken, we would draw attention to the residences of the Royal Family and the Prince of Liège, and also to the Chinese Pavilion, the Japanese Tower, and the Royal greenhouses.

Front des Königlichen Museums für Schöne Künste.

Der klassizistische Königsplatz datiert vom Ende des 18. Jahrhunderts (typischer Ludwig XVI.-Stil). Er kann in seiner strengen Schönheit mit verschiedenen französischen Plätzen aufnehmen. Der Platz wird beherrscht durch den Giebel der St Jakob - auf - dem - Kaltenberg-Kirche. In der Mitte erhebt sich das Denkmal Gottfrieds von Bouillon. Unter einer Bogenreihe kommt man auf den stillen Museumsplatz mit der Königl. Bibliothek und dem Museum für Moderne Kunst, dem früheren Palast Herzog Karls von Lothringen. Vom Königsplatz ist es nur ein Schritt nach dem Palästeplatz, der gelegen ist zwischen dem grünen Stadtpark, dem breit hingelagertem Königsschloss (Beginn 20. Jh.) und der klassizistischen Front des Akademienpalasts. In der Rue de la Loi befinden sich das Parlament und verschiedene Ministerien, die ein reizvolles Ganzes in Ludwig XVI.-Stil bilden. Im Hintergrund wird der Horizont abgeschlossen durch das Siegestor des Jubelparks (1905). Wenn wir die Königsstrasse hinuntergehen, erreichen wir zuerst die Kongressäule (1850-59) mit dem Grab des Unbekannten Soldaten. Weitergehend, vorbei am ehemaligen Botanischen Garten, liegt die Ste Mariakirche. Etwas davor, an der grossen Kreuzung, können wir links in der Ferne die Nationalbasilika von Koekelberg auftauchen sehen. Die Suche nach Monumenten und touristischen Sehenswürdigkeiten endigen wir mit einem Spaziergang längs der Mittelallee. Dort sehen wir im Vorbeigehen auf dem Brouckèreplatz das Anspach-Denkmal und etwas weiter weg die Börse (1875).

Brüssel hat viele Museen aller Art, das Museum der Schönen Künste, der Archäologie, der Musik, der Ethnologie und der Naturgeschichte.

In den Randgebieten von Brüssel müssen noch erwähnt werden : das Museum für Zentralafrika in Tervuren, das Erasmushaus in Anderlecht; auf der anderen Seite der Stadt in Laken richten wir den Blick auf die Residenz des Königs, das Schloss des Prinzen von Lüttich, den Chinesischen Pavillon, den Japanischen Turm, die königl. Gewächshäuser und das Atomium.

GAND

L'ancienne capitale de la Flandre n'a rien à envier à ses sœurs belges quant à la richesse de son patrimoine historique. Au centre de la ville le visiteur sera même ébloui par une suite de monuments dont l'enfilade est unique au monde : l'église Saint-Michel (XVe siècle), l'église Saint-Nicolas (XIIIe siècle), le beffroi (XIIIe-XIVe siècles) avec les halles et l'annexe baroque du « Mammelokker », et la cathédrale Saint-Bavon (XIIIe-XIVe siècle) où est conservé le polyptyque de l'Agneau Mystique des frères Van Eyck. Non loin de là, se trouve le marché aux Grains aux pignons historiques qui donnent un résumé de l'architecture civile flamande aux siècles passés, le style roman y voisine avec les styles gothique et Renaissance. A côté de l'église Saint-Michel, se trouvent les vestiges d'un ancien couvent des dominicains, appelé le « Pand ». Derrière la cathédrale Saint-Bavon, s'érige le Steen ou hôtel de Gérard le Diable (XIIIe siècle). D'autres demeures patriciennes remarquables sont la Faucille et l'Arrière-Faucille, l'hôtel d'Hane-Steenhuyse, l'hôtel Faligan, etc. Au chapitre de l'architecture civile, Gand possède cependant d'autres raisons d'orgueil : le château des Comtes qui date, en ses parties principales, de la fin du XIIe siècle. L'hôtel de ville, fort remarquable, est en partie en style gothique et en partie en style Renaissance. Gand possède en outre les vestiges des grandes abbayes de la Bylok, de Saint-Bavon, de Saint-Pierre et de Baudeloo, ainsi que deux béguinages. Parmi les monuments de style moderne, citons la tour de la bibliothèque de l'université. Gand est riche en musées divers: beaux-arts, archéologie et folklore. Tous méritent une visite attentive car tous abondent en chefs-d'œuvre ou en objets du plus haut intérêt.

GENT

De voormalige hoofdstad van Vlaanderen heeft haar Belgische zustersteden niets te benijden voor wat de rijkdom van haar historisch patrimonium betreft. In het stadscentrum wordt de toerist getroffen door de opeenvolging van een reeks monumenten, die enig zijn ter wereld : de Sint-Michielskerk (15de eeuw), de Sint-Niklaaskerk (13de eeuw), het Belfort (13de-14de eeuw) met de Hallen en het barokbijgebouw van de Mammelokker, de Sint-Baafskathedraal (13de-14de eeuw), waar Van Eyck's polyptiek 'Het Lam Gods' wordt bewaard. Niet ver vandaar ligt de Korenmarkt met haar krans van historische voorgevels, die als het ware een samenvatting vormen van de Vlaamse burgerlijke bouwkunde van vroeger eeuwen en waar men de romaanse stijl aantreft naast de gotiek en de renaissance. Bij de Sint-Michielskerk zien wij de overblijfselen van een oud Dominikanerklooster, ook het 'Pand' genoemd. Achter de Sint-Baafskathedraal verrijst het Geeraard-Duivelsteen (13de eeuw). Merkwaardige patriciërswoningen zijn de Sikkel en de Achter-Sikkel, evenals de herenwoningen d'Hane-Steenhuyse, Faligan e.a. Op het gebied van de burgerlijke bouwkunde heeft Gent nog andere redenen om trots te zijn : o.m. op het Gravenkasteel, waarvan de hoofdgedeelten opklimmen tot het einde van de 12de eeuw, evenals op het mooie stadhuis dat gedeeltelijk in gotische en gedeeltelijk in renaissance-stijl is opgetrokken. Te Gent vindt men de overblijfselen van de grote abdijen van Byloke en van Sint-Baafs, van Sint-Pieter en van Baudelo, evenals twee begijnhoven. Tot de monumenten in moderne stijl behoort de toren van de Universiteitsbibliotheek. Gent bezit verschillende musea : schone kunsten, archeologie en folklore. Alle verdienen zij een aandachtig bezoek want zij zijn zeer rijk aan meesterwerken of aan merkwaardige verzamelingen.

GHENT

The old capital city of Flanders is as rich in art treasures as the other main towns in the country. In the centre of the city, the visitor will be amazed by the alignement of monuments, forming a unique pattern: the St. Michael church (15th century), the St. Nicolas church (13th century), the belfry (13th-15th centuries), with the covered market and the baroque "Mammelokker" annexe, and the St. Bavon cathedral (13th-14th centureis) which houses the polyptych of the Mystical Lamb by the Van Eyck brothers. Nearby, the Grain market is located, with the historic façades offering a survey of Flemish civil architecture in the past centuries, from romanesque to gothic and Renaissance features. Next to the St. Michael church are the remains of an old dominican convent, called the "Pand". Behind St. Bavon cathedral, there is the Steen, or residence of Gérard le Diable (13th century). Other patrician residences include the Faucille and the Arrière-Faucille, the d'Hane-Steenhuyse house, the Faligan residence, etc. With regard to civil architecture, Ghent is specially proud of its château des Comtes, the main parts of which were erected at the end of the 12th century. The remarkable city hall is partly in gothic, partly in Renaissance style. Ghent further has remains of a number of major abbeys: Byloke, St. Bavon, St. Pierre and Baudeloo, and two beguine convents. Among the modern buildings, the tower of the University Library stands out. Ghent has several museums: fine arts, archeology, and folk-lore. All deserve a visit and attention, for they are full of masterpieces, or highly interesting objects.

GENT

Die frühere Hauptstadt Flanderns hat ein eben reiches Erbgut als ihre belgischen Schwesternstädte.

Im Stadtzentrum wird man überrascht durch die Aufeinanderfolge von Sehenswürdigkeiten, die auf der Welt einzigartig sind : die St. Michaelskirche (15. Jh.), die St. Nikolauskirche (13. Jh.), den Belfried (13.-14. Jh.) mit den Hallen und die St. Bavokathedrale (13.-14. Jh.), wo das Polyptychon »Die Anbetung des Lammes« von Van Eyck aufbewahrt wird. Nicht weit entfernt liegt der Korenmarkt (Getreidemarkt) in einem Kranz historischer Giebel, die geradezu eine Zusammenfassung der flämischen bürgerlichen Architektur früherer Jahrhunderte bilden und wo man den romanischen Stil neben der Gotik und Renaissance antrifft. Bei der Michaelskirche sehen wir die Reste eines alten Dominikanerklosters, das »Pand« genannt. Hinter der Bavokathedrale erhebt sich das Geerard Duivelschloss (13. Jh.). Bemerkenswerte Patrizierhäuser sind »De Sikkel« und »De Achtersikkel« ebenso die Herrenhäuser d'Hane-Steenhuyse, Faligan u.a. Ganz besonders stolz kann Gent auf seine Grafenburg sein (Gravensteen, kurz »Steen« genannt), dessen Hauptteile im 12. Jahrhundert entstanden sind. Das sehr schöne Rathaus ist teils gotisch teils im Renaissancestil erbaut worden. Es gibt auch noch Reste der grossen Abteien von Bijloke, St. Bavo, St. Peter und von Baudelo; auch bestehen noch die zwei Beginenhöfe.

Zur modernen Architektur gehören der Turm der Universitätsbibliothek. Gent besitzt verschiedene Museen : für bildende Kunst, Archäologie und Volkskunde. Alle verdienen sie einem aufmerksamen Besuch; sie sind reich an Meisterwerken und bedeutenden Sammlungen.

LIÈGE

Liège, la Cité Ardente aux portes de l'Ardenne, recèle maints témoignages de son glorieux passé, dont les églises Saint-Denis, Saint-Barthélemy (surtout célèbre par les fonds baptismaux de Renier de Huy), la cathédrale Saint-Jacques, l'église Saint-Jean (avec le reliquaire de Charles le Téméraire) et l'église Sainte-Croix (XIIIe siècle). Sur les hauteurs de Cointe, la ville est

LUIK

Luik, de 'Cité ardente', in de onmiddellijke nabijheid van de Ardennen, bewaart vele getuigenissen van haar glorierijk verleden, waaronder de kerken van Sint-Dionisius, Sint-Bartholomeus (vooral beroemd om de doopvont van Reinier van Hoei), de Sint-Jacobskathedraal, de Sint-Janskerk (met het votiefbeeld van Karel de Stoute), en de Heilig-Kruiskerk (13de eeuw). Op de

LIÈGE

Liège, the "Cité Ardente" on the threshold of the Ardennes, is full of testimonials of the city's glorious past, e.g. the St. Denis and St. Barthélemy churches (the latter famous for its baptismal font by Renier de Huy), the St. James cathedral, the St. John church (with the shrine of Charles the Bold) and the Ste. Croix church (13th century). On the Cointe hills, a modern

LÜTTICH

Lüttich, die unruhige Stadt in der unmittelbaren Nähe der Ardennen, bewahrt viele Zeugen ihrer rühmlichen Vergangenheit. Darunter fallen die Kirchen von St Dionisius, St Bartholomäus (die vor allem berühmt ist wegen des Taufbeckens von Reiner von Huy, die St Jakobskathedrale, die St Janskirche (mit dem Weihgeschenk von Karl dem Kühnen) und die Hl. Kreuzkirche

dominée par une basilique moderne et le monument interallié. Dans le domaine de l'architecture civile, la Cité Ardente s'enorgueillit de posséder un des plus beaux monuments Renaissance de la Belgique, le palais des Princes-Évêques (XVIe siècle). Elle possède un bel hôtel de ville et un perron du XVIIIe siècle, de même que de fort belles demeures patriciennes dont la Maison Curtius et l'hôtel d'Ansembourg. Liège est d'autre part fière de ses fontaines monumentales de même que de son Musée Grétry. Liège possède également de très riches musées dont le Musée de la Vie wallonne.

heuvel van Cointe verheft zich een moderne basiliek en het monument van de geallieerden.

Op het gebied van de burgerlijke bouwkunst kan Luik bogen op een van de mooiste renaissance-monumenten van België, namelijk het paleis der Prins-Bisschoppen (16de eeuw). De stad bezit een mooi stadhuis, een Perron uit de 18de eeuw en mooie patricierswoningen, waaronder deze van Curtius en van Ansembourg. Luik bezit ook monumentale fonteinen alsook een klein Grétry-museum. Evenals in de andere Belgische kunststeden treffen wij ook hier rijke musea aan, waaronder dat van het Waalse Leven, dat een ware synthese is van de Waalse folklore.

basilica and a monument to the Allies command the view of the city. In the sector of civil architecture, Liège takes pride in possessing one of Belgium's finest Renaissance monuments: the Palace of the Prince-Bishops (16th century). The city also has a fine city hall, a "perron" (18th century), and some very beautiful patrician residences, such as Curtius House and the Ansembourg residence. Liège also is proud of its monumental fountains, and of its Grétry museum. The city also has very interesting museums, i.a. the Museum of Walloon Life.

(13. Jh.), auf dem Cointehügel erhebt sich eine moderne Basilika und das Denkmal der Gefallenen.

Die »Unruhige Stadt« ist sehr stolz, dass sie das schönste Renaissancegebäude Belgiens besitzt, nl. der Fürstbischöfliche Palast (16. Jh.). Die Stadt hat ein schönes Rathaus, einen Perron aus dem 18. Jahrhundert und schöne Patrizierhäuser, darunter die von Curtius und Ansembourg. Lüttich ist stolz auf seine monumentalen Brunnen und sein hübsches Grétymuseum.

Ebenso wie in den anderen belgischen Kunststädten treffen wir hier reiche Museen an, so z.B. das Museum des wallonischen Lebens.

MONS

L'ancienne capitale du comté du Hainaut possède encore quelques vestiges de l'ancienne résidence comtale qui sont du XIIIe siècle, alors que la chapelle Saint-Calixte date même du XIe siècle. Mais Mons s'enorgueillit surtout de sa collégiale Sainte-Waudru (XVe siècle), de son hôtel de ville (XVe siècle) et de son beffroi en style baroque. Le touriste visitera également l'église Saint-Nicolas (XVIIIe siècle), la chapelle Sainte-Marguerite (XIIIe siècle), la Conciergerie ou prison scabinale, ainsi que plusieurs musées fort intéressants dont celui du chanoine Puissant (archéologie), celui d'histoire naturelle et celui de la vie montoise.

BERGEN

De voormalige hoofdstad van het graafschap Henegouwen bezit enkele overblijfselen van de vroegere grafelijke residentie en wel uit de 13de eeuw, waaronder de Sint-Calixtuskapel, die zelfs uit de 11de eeuw zou dateren. Bergen is fier op zijn collegiale kerk van Sint-Waltrudis (15de eeuw), zijn stadhuis (15de eeuw) en zijn Belfort in barokstijl. De toerist mag niet verzuimen een bezoek te brengen aan de Sint-Niklaaskerk (18de eeuw), aan de Sint-Margaretha kapel (13de eeuw), aan de Conciergerie (gevangenis van de voormalige schepenbank) en aan verschillende belangrijke musea, waaronder dat van kanunnik Puissant (archeologie) en aan deze voor natuurhistorie en plaatselijke folklore.

MONS

The old capital of county Hainaut still has some 13th century vestiges of the counts' residence. The St. Calixte chapel even dates from the 11th century. Mons, however, features primarily its St. Waudru collegiate church (15th century), its city hall (15th century), and its baroque belfry. The tourist also will visit the St. Nicholas church (18th century), the St. Marguerite chapel (13th century), the Conciergerie or Bailiff's jail, and several very interesting museums, i.a. the canon Puissant museum of archeology, the museums of natural history, and of the history and life of the city.

MONS

Die frühere Hauptstadt der Grafschaft Hainaut besitzt einige Ruinen der früheren gräflichen Residenz (13. Jh.), wozu auch die St Calixtuskapelle gehört, die allerdings aus dem 11. Jahrhundert datieren soll. Mons ist stolz auf seine St Waltrudiskirche (15. Jh.), sein Rathaus (15. Jh.) und seinen barocken Belfried.

Auch ein Besuch der St Nikolauskirche (18. Jh.), der Ste Margaretakapelle (13. Jh.) der Conciergerie oder des Gefängnisses der früheren Schöffenbank ist sehr lohnend. Auch hier gibt es wichtige Museen, darunter das des Kanoniker Puissant (Archäologie), das Naturkunde- und das Folkloremuseum.

NAMUR

L'ancienne capitale du comté de Namur recèle des richesses artistiques de tout premier plan : la cathédrale Saint-Aubin, de style baroque, les églises Saint-Loup en néo-classique, Notre-Dame, Saint-Joseph et Saint-Jean ; il y a ensuite l'hôtel de ville (1828) et le beffroi (XIVe siècle), généralement appelé tour Saint-Jacques. N'oublions point ni le pont de Jambes ni une demi-douzaine de musées historiques, archéologiques et forestier. Parmi les principaux trésors d'art namurois, citons les œuvres d'orfèvrerie romane d'Hugo d'Oignies conservées au petit musée du couvent des Sœurs de Notre-Dame, ainsi que les richesses du remarquable Musée archéologique.

NAMEN

De oude hoofdplaats van het graafschap Namen bezit enkele kunstschatten van eerste rang : de Sint-Albanuskathedraal (barok), de Sint-Lupuskerk (neo-classicisme), Onze-Lieve-Vrouw, Sint-Jozef en Sint-Jan ; daarnaast het stadhuis en het Belfort (14de eeuw), dat algemeen bekend staat als de Sint-Jacobstoren. Wij noemen eveneens de brug van Jambes, modern kultureel centrum aan de samenvloeiing van Maas en Samber, en een zestal musea : geschiedenis, archeologie en bosbouw. Tot de voornaamste Naamse kunstschatten behoren de romaanse kunstscheppingen van de edelsmid Hugo d'Oignies, die bewaard worden in het klooster van de zusters van Onze-Lieve-Vrouw, en de rijkdommen van het merkwaardige archeologische museum.

NAMUR

The one-time capital of the county Namur has first class artistic treasures: the St. Aubin cathedral, in baroque style, the neo-classical St. Loup church, and those devoted to Notre-Dame, St. Joseph and St. John. Further, there are the city hall (1828), and the belfry (14th century) usually called Tour St. Jacques. One should not forget the bridge at Jambes and include also several historical, archeological and forestry museums. Among Namur's most precious art treasures, there are the romanesque gold plate works by Hugo d'Oignies, kept in the small museum of the Sisters of Notre-Dame convent, and the valuable collection in het museum of archeology.

NAMUR

Die alte Hauptstadt der Grafschaft Namur besitzt einige Kunstschätze ersten Ranges : die St. Albanuskathedrale (Barock), die St Lupuskirche (Neuklassismus), die Frauenkirche, St Joseph und St Janskirche, dann noch das Rathaus und den Belfried (14. Jh.), allgemein bekannt als St Jakobsturm. Erwähnenswert sind noch die Pont-de-Jambes (Jambes, ein modernes Zentrum am Zusammenfluss von Maas und Sambre), und noch einige Museen für Geschichte, Archäologie und Forstbau. Zu den besonderen Kunstschätzen Namurs gehören die romanischen Schöpfungen des Edelschmieds Hugo d'Oignies, die das Kloster der Nonnen von U.L.Frau bewahrt, und auch die Reichtümer des bemerkenswerten archäologischen Museums.

TOURNAI

Tournai, l'ancienne capitale du royaume franc, se distingue surtout par cet incomparable chef-d'œuvre d'architecture romane et gothique qu'est la cathédrale aux cinq clochers. Gravement endommagé au début de la guerre 1940-45, Tournai n'en possède pas moins nombre d'autres monuments remarquables : un beffroi du XIIᵉ siècle (le plus ancien de Belgique), le pont des Trous (XIIIᵉ siècle), les tours Marvis (XIIIᵉ siècle) et Henri VIII (XVIᵉ siècle), tous trois vestiges des fortifications de la ville, ainsi que plusieurs églises : Saint-Quentin, Saint-Jacques, Saint-Piat (XIIIᵉ siècle), Sainte-Marguerite, Sainte-Marie-Madeleine, Saint-Nicolas et Saint-Brice (XIIᵉ siècle) dont plusieurs ont dû être sérieusement restaurées, voire même reconstruites. La ville compte d'autre part nombre de maisons anciennes en styles roman et gothique, mais surtout des XVIIᵉ et XVIIIᵉ siècles. Tournai est également riche en musées de tous genres, mais c'est surtout son nouveau Musée des Beaux-Arts qui retiendra l'attention en raison de la richesse de ses collections. Le trésor de la cathédrale, lui aussi, mérite une visite attentive.

DOORNIK

Doornik, de oude hoofdstad van het Frankische rijk, imponeert door een onvergelijkelijk meesterwerk van romaanse en gotische bouwkunst, namelijk de kathedraal met haar vijf torens. Hoewel erg gehavend tijdens de oorlog 1940-45, heeft Doornik nochtans talrijke andere historische gebouwen ongeschonden bewaard : een belfort uit de 12de eeuw (het oudste van België), de 'Pont des Trous' (13de eeuw), de 'Tour Marvis' (13de eeuw) en de toren van Hendrik de Achtste (16de eeuw) – deze laatste drie torens zijn de overblijfselen van de vroegere versterkingen van de stad – en verscheidene kerken o.m. die van Saint-Quentin, Saint-Jacques, Saint-Piat (13de eeuw), Sainte-Marguerite, Sainte-Marie-Madeleine, Saint-Nicolas en Sainte-Brice (12de eeuw), waarvan verscheidene grondig gerestaureerd en zelfs herbouwd werden. De stad telt talrijke oude woningen in romaanse en gotische stijl, maar vooral uit de 17de en de 18de eeuw. Doornik is rijk aan musea van alle aard. Het bezit o.m. een nieuw museum voor schone kunsten, belangrijk omwille van de rijkdom zijner verzamelingen. Ook de kunstschatten van de kathedraal zijn een aandachtig bezoek overwaard.

TOURNAI

Tournai, once the capital of the Frankish Kingdom, is famous for the incomparable beauty of its cathedral church, with its five towers,—a building partly in romanesque, partly in gothic style. Although severly damaged in the early days of the 1940-1945 war, Tournai possesses some other remarkable monuments, including a 13th century belfry (the oldest one in Belgium), the "pont des Trous" (13th century) the towers Marvis (13th century) and Henri VIII (16th century)—the latter three being remains of the city's fortifications—, and a series of churches: St. Quentin, St. James, St. Piat (13th century), St. Margaret, St. Marie-Madeleine, St. Nicholas, St. Brice (12th century). Several of the latter had to be restored, or even rebuilt. The city also has a number of old, romanesque or gothic, houses, and many residences dating from the 17th and 18th centuries. Tournai further features several museums, among which the museum of Fine Arts is outstanding because of the wealth of its collections. The cathedral's treasury also deserves a leisurely visit.

TOURNAI

Tournai, die alte Hauptstadt des Fränkischen Reiches, imponiert durch ein unvergleichliches Meisterwerk der romanischen und gotischen Baukunst, die Kathedrale mit fünf Türmen. Obwohl die Stadt im zweiten Weltkrieg sehr beschädigt wurde, hat Tournai noch zahlreiche historische Gebäude, die unversehrt blieben : einen Belfried (12. Jh., der älteste Belgiens), die »Pont des Trous« (13. Jh.), den »Tour Marvis« (13. Jh.) und die »Türme Heinrichs VIII. (16. Jh.). Diese drei Türme sind das einzige was erhalten geblieben ist von den früheren Befestigungen der Stadt) und verschiedene Kirchen, darunter : St Quentin, St Jakob, St Piat (13. Jh.), Ste Marguerite, Ste Maria-Madeleine, St Nikolaus und St Brice (12. Jh.). Einige von ihnen sind gründlich restauriert oder wieder neu erbaut worden. Die Stadt hat zahlreiche alte Häuser in romanischem und gotischem Stil, auch viele aus dem 17. und 18. Jahrhundert. Tournai ist reich an Museen aller Art. Besonders das neue Museum für schöne Kunst verdient Interesse, wegen seiner reichen Sammlungen. Auch die Kunstschätze der Kathedrale lohnen durchaus einen Besuch.

LES AUTRES VILLES D'ART

Le périple des sept grandes villes d'art belges terminé, passons encore rapidement en revue les principales richesses de quelques autres.

Voici tout d'abord, dans l'ordre alphabétique : AARSCHOT, et son église Notre-Dame (XIVᵉ siècle) au beau jubé et son hôtel de ville (XVᵉ siècle); ALOST, et son église Saint-Martin (XVᵉ siècle), son beffroi (1200), son hôtel communal (XIVᵉ siècle) et son hôtel de ville néoclassique; AUDENARDE, au splendide hôtel de ville (XVIᵉ siècle) et ses églises Notre-Dame de Pamele (XIIIᵉ siècle) et Sainte-Walburge (XIIIᵉ-XIVᵉ siècles); BINCHE, au fameux carnaval, avec ses remparts et son hôtel de ville; COURTRAI, et son beffroi (XIVᵉ siècle), son hôtel de ville (XVIᵉ siècle), ses églises Notre-Dame (XIVᵉ siècle) et Saint-Martin, ainsi que ses Broeltorens; DAMME, ancien avant-port de Bruges, avec son église monumentale (XIIIᵉ-XIVᵉ siècles) et son hôtel de ville (XVᵉ siècle); DIEST, et son église Saint-Sulpice (XVᵉ siècle), ses halles (XIVᵉ siècle), et son hôtel de ville (XVIIIᵉ siècle); DIXMUDE, avec son église

DE ANDERE KUNSTSTEDEN

Na dit bezoek aan de zeven grote Belgische kunststeden komt de beurt aan enkele steden die interessante kunstschatten bezitten.

Ze volgen hier alfabetisch gerangschikt: AALST met de Sint-Martinuskerk (15de eeuw), het belfort (12de eeuw), het gemeentehuis (14de eeuw) en het neo-klassieke stadhuis; AARSCHOT: de Onze-Lieve-Vrouwkerk (14de eeuw) met prachtig oksaal en het stadhuis (15de eeuw); BINCHE met het befaamde karnaval, de oude vestingen en het stadhuis; DAMME, de vroegere voorhaven van Brugge, met zijn monumentale kerk (13de-14de eeuw) en het stadhuis (15de eeuw); DENDERMONDE met zijn stadhuis (15de eeuw), de collegiale kerk van Onze-Lieve-Vrouw (14de eeuw), het begijnhof en het moderne gerechtshof; DIEST met de Sint-Sulpiciuskerk (15de eeuw), de hallen (14de eeuw), het stadhuis (18de eeuw) en het unieke begijnhof; DIKSMUIDE met de Sint-Martinuskerk (14de eeuw) en het stadhuis (14de eeuw), beide heropgebouwd na de oorlog 1914-18; HALLE, met de basiliek van Onze-Lieve-Vrouw

OTHER ART CENTRES

Now that we have reviewed the country's seven main art centres, let us take a brief look at the riches in some of the other cities.

Taking them more or less in alphabetical order, we first come to AARSCHOT, with its Notre-Dame church (14th century—it has a fine rood-screen), and city hall (15th century); AALST, and its St. Martin church (15th century) and belfry (1200), its town hostel (14th century), and neo-classical city hall; OUDENAARDE, its splendid city hall, its Notre-Dame de Pamele (13th century), and St. Walburge churches; BINCHE, with its celebrated carnival, its ramparts and city hall; KORTRIJK, its belfry (14th century), city hall (16th century), its Notre-Dame (14th century) and St. Martin churches and its Broel-towers; DAMME, Bruges's former outer harbour, with its monumental church (13th-14th centuries) and town hall (15th century); DIEST, and its St. Sulpice church (15th century), its covered market (14th century) and city hall (15th century); DIKSMUIDE, with its St. Nicholas church (14th

DIE ANDEREN KUNSTSTÄDTE

Nach Besichtigung der sieben grossen Kunststädte nennen wir einige andere Städte, die interessante Kunstwerke besitzen. Sie folgen hier alphabetisch geordnet:
AALST mit seiner St Martinuskirche (15. Jh.), seinem Belfried (12. Jh.) und dem Gemeindehaus (14. Jh.) und dem neuklassizistischen Rathaus. AARSCHOT mit der Frauenkirche (14. Jh.) und Rathaus (15. Jh.). BINCHE mit seinem berühmten Karneval, alten Festungen und Rathaus. DAMME, dem früheren Vorhafen von Brügge, mit seiner monumentalen Kirche (13.-14. Jh.) und seinem Rathaus (15. Jh.). DENDERMONDE mit seinem Rathaus (15. Jh.), seiner Frauenkirche (14. Jh.), dem Beginenhof und dem modernen Gerichtshof. DIEST mit der St Sulpiciuskirche (15. Jh.), den Hallen (14. Jh.) und dem Rathaus (18. Jh.). DIKSMUIDE mit St Martinuskirche (14. Jh.) und Rathaus (14. Jh.), beide nach dem 1. Weltkrieg wieder aufgebaut. HALLE mit der Frauenbasilika (14. Jh.). HASSELT, die Hauptstadt der Provinz Limburg mit seiner St Quintinuskirche (15.

French

Saint-Nicolas (XIVᵉ siècle) et son hôtel de ville (XIVᵉ siècle), tous deux reconstruits après la guerre 1914-1918; FURNES, avec ses églises Sainte-Walburge et Saint-Nicolas (XVᵉ siècle), son hôtel de ville Renaissance et son beffroi (1618); HAL, et sa basilique Notre-Dame (XIVᵉ siècle); HASSELT, capitale du Limbourg, avec son église Saint-Quentin (XVᵉ siècle) et son béguinage; HUY, et sa collégiale et sa citadelle, toutes deux déjà citées; LÉAU, et son église Saint-Léonard (XIVᵉ-XVᵉ siècles) et son hôtel de ville; LOUVAIN, et son hôtel de ville (XVᵉ siècle), sa collégiale Saint-Pierre (XIVᵉ-XVᵉ siècles), ses églises Sainte-Gertrude (XIIIᵉ siècle), Saint-Jacques (XIIIᵉ siècle), Saint-Michel (XVIIᵉ siècle), son béguinage, ses halles aux Draps (XIVᵉ siècle) et ses bâtiments universitaires, dont la bibliothèque; MALINES, sa cathédrale Saint-Rombaut (XVᵉ siècle) et ses églises dont celle de Notre-Dame-au-delà-de-la-Dyle (XVᵉ siècle), Notre-Dame d'Hanswyck (XVIIᵉ siècle), Saint-Jean et Saint-Pierre, et sa porte de Bruxelles; MONTAIGU et sa basilique (XVIIᵉ siècle); NIEUPORT, et son église Notre-Dame, ses halles et son hôtel de ville reconstruits après la guerre 1914-1918; NIVELLES, sa collégiale Sainte-Gertrude et son cloître roman; RENAIX, et son église Saint-Hermès; SAINT-TROND, et sa grand-place avec hôtel de ville, beffroi et collégiale Notre-Dame; SOIGNIES, et sa collégiale Saint-Vincent (XIᵉ siècle); TERMONDE, et son hôtel de ville (XVᵉ siècle), sa collégiale Notre-Dame (XIVᵉ siècle), son béguinage et son palais de justice moderne; TIRLEMONT, et son église Notre-Dame-au-Lac; TONGRES, avec ses vestiges de remparts romains, son église Notre-Dame (XVᵉ siècle), son cloître roman et son béguinage; WALCOURT et son église gothique; YPRES, et ses halles, sa cathédrale Saint-Martin, ses églises Saint-Jacques, Saint-Pierre et Saint-Nicolas ainsi que sa porte de Menin. Tous ces monuments reconstruits après la guerre 1914-1918.

Dutch

(14de eeuw); HASSELT, hoofdplaats van Limburg, met zijn Sint-Quintinuskerk (15de eeuw) en het begijnhof; HOEI, met zijn collegiale kerk en de citadel; IEPER met de alombekende hallen, de Sint-Martinuskathedraal (13de eeuw), de kerken van Sint-Jacob, Sint-Pieter en Sint-Nikolaas en de Meense Poort, alle na de oorlog 1914-18 heropgebouwd; KORTRIJK met zijn belfort (14de eeuw), stadhuis (16de eeuw), de kerken van Onze-Lieve-Vrouw (14de eeuw) en van Sint-Martinus en de Broeltorens; LEUVEN met het stadhuis (15de eeuw), de collegiale Sint-Pieterskerk (14de-15de eeuw), de Sint-Gertrudiskerk (13de eeuw), de Sint-Jacobskerk (13de eeuw), de Sint-Michielskerk (17de eeuw), het begijnhof, de lakenhallen (14de eeuw) en de universiteitsgebouwen, waaronder de bibliotheek; MECHELEN en zijn Sint-Romboutskathedraal (15de eeuw), de kerken van Onze-Lieve-Vrouw-over-de-Dijle (15de eeuw), Onze-Lieve-Vrouw van Hanswijk (17de eeuw), Sint-Jan en Sint-Pieter en de Brusselse Poort; NIEUWPOORT met zijn Onze-Lieve-Vrouwkerk, hallen en stadhuis, die na de oorlog 1914-18 werden heropgebouwd; NIJVEL met zijn collegiale Sint-Geertruikerk en klooster, beide in romaanse stijl; OUDENAARDE met zijn prachtig stadhuis (16de eeuw) en de kerken Onze-Lieve-Vrouw-van-Pamele (12de eeuw) en Sint-Walburgis (13de-14de eeuw); RONSE, met de Sint-Hermeskerk; SCHERPENHEUVEL met zijn basiliek (17de eeuw); SINT-TRUIDEN met zijn Grote Markt en zijn stadhuis, het belfort en de collegiale Onze-Lieve-Vrouwkerk; TIENEN met zijn kerk van Onze-Lieve-Vrouw-ter-Poel; TONGEREN met de overblijfselen van Romeinse vestingwerken, de Onze-Lieve-Vrouwkerk (15de eeuw), het romaans klooster en het begijnhof; VEURNE, met de kerken van Sint-Walburgis en Sint-Niklaas (15de eeuw), zijn renaissance stadhuis en het belfort (1618); WALCOURT met zijn gotische kerk; ZINNIK met de collegiale Sint-Vincentiuskerk (11de eeuw); ZOUTLEEUW met zijn Sint-Leonarduskerk (14de-15de eeuw), hallen (15de eeuw) en stadhuis.

English

century) and city hall (14th century),—both rebuilt after the 1914-1918 war; VEURNE, with its St. Walburge and St. Nicholas churches (XVth century), its Renaissance city hall, and belfry (1618); HALLE, and its Notre-Dame basilica (14th century); HASSELT, capital of Limburg, with its St. Quentin church (15th century) and beguine convent; ZOUTLEEUW, its St. Leonard church (14th-15th centuries), and town hall; LEUVEN, its city hall (15th century) its collegiate church St. Peter (14th-15th centuries), its St. Gertrude (13th century), St. James (13th century) and St. Michael (17th century) churches, its beguine convent, its covered cloth market (14th century) and its University buildings, e.g. the library; MECHELEN, its St. Rombaut cathedral (15th century) and churches, Notre-Dame-beyond-the-Dyle (15th century), Notre-Dame d'Hanswyck Peter, and its Brussels gateway; SCHERPENHEUVEL, and its basilica (17th century); NIEUWPOORT, its Notre-Dame church, covered market and city hall, all rebuilt after the 1914-1918 war; RONSE, and its St. Hermes church; ST. TRUIDEN, its market place with town hall, belfry and collegiate church Notre-Dame; SOIGNIES, and its St. Vincent collegiate church (11th century); DENDERMONDE, its city hall (15th century), Notre-Dame collegiate church, beguine convent, and contemporary court of justice; TIENEN, and its Notre-Dame-au-Lac church; TONGEREN, with its remnants of Roman ramparts, its Notre-Dame church (15th century), its romanesque cloisters and beguine convent; WALCOURT, and its gothic church; IEPEREN, its covered markets, St. Martin cathedral, St. James, St. Peter and St. Nicholas churches, and its Menin gateway. All these monuments were rebuilt after the 1914-1918 war.

German

Jh.) und dem Beginenhof. HUY mit der imposanten Kirche und der Zitadelle. IEPER mit dem berühmten Hallen, der St Martinuskathedrale (13. Jh.), St. Jakob und St. Peter, der St Nikolauskirche und der Menense Poort (alle diese Gebäude sind nach dem Krieg 14/18 wieder aufgebaut worden). KORTRIJK mit dem Belfried (14. Jh.), dem Rathaus (16. Jh.), der Frauenkirche (14. Jh.) und der St Martinuskirche, den Broeltürmen. LÖWEN mit Rathaus (15. Jh.), St Peterskirche (14.-15. Jh.), Ste Gertrudiskirche (13. Jh.), St Jakobskirche (13. Jh.), St Michaelskirche (17. Jh.), Beginenhof, Tuchhalle (14. Jh.) und den Universitätsgebäuden, mit der Bibliothek. MECHELEN mit der St Romboutskathedrale (15. Jh.), den Kirchen U.L.Frau-über-die-Dijle (15. Jh.), U.L.Frau-von-Hanswijk (17. Jh.), St Johannes und St Peter und der Brusseler Poort. NIEUWPOORT mit Frauenkirche, den Hallen und dem Rathaus, die nach dem Kriege 14/18 wieder aufgebaut wurden. NIVELLES mit der Gertruikirche und dem Kloster, beides in romanischem Stil. OUDENAARDE mit den prächtigen Rathaus (16. Jh.) und den Kirchen von U.L.Frau-von-Pamele (12. Jh.) und der Ste Walburgis (13.-14. Jh.). RONSE mit der St Hermeskirche. SCHERPENHEUVEL mit seiner Basilika (17. Jh.). SINT-TRUIDEN mit dem Grossen Markt und dem Rathaus, dem Belfried und der Frauenkirche. SOIGNIES mit der St Vincentiuskirche (11. Jh.). TIENEN mit der U.L.Frau-ter-Poelkirche. TONGEREN mit den Ruinen der Festungsanlagen aus der Römerzeit, der Frauenkirche (15. Jh.), dem romanischen Kloster und dem Beginenhof. VEURNE mit Ste Walburgis und St Nikolauskirche (15 .Jh.), dem Renaissancerathaus und dem Belfried (1618). WALCOURT mit gotischer Kirche. ZOUTLEEUW mit St Leonarduskirche (14.-15. Jh.), den Hallen (15. Jh.) und dem Rathaus.

LE FOLKLORE

Le folklore de la Belgique est aussi riche que varié. Il rythme le déroulement des jours fastes sans cesse renouvelés. Au début de l'année se succèdent les multiples fêtes de carnaval qui commencent dès le samedi précédant le Mardi-Gras et qui se prolongent jusqu'au Laetare.

DE FOLKLORE

De folklore van België is even rijk als verscheiden. Zij symboliseert de kring van de steeds weerkomende feestdagen. In 't begin van het jaar worden talrijke karnavalfeesten gevierd die beginnen op de zaterdag vóór Vastenavond en duren tot Rozenzondag. Tot de meest typische

BELGIAN FOLKLORE

Belgium's folk-lore is both abundant and varied. It marks the festive succession of never-ending celebrations. Early in the year, carnival festivities are spread, from the Saturday preceding Shrove Tuesday until Laetare Sunday. We mention, among many others: Eupen's Rosen-

DIE FOLKLORE

Die belgische Folklore ist reich und verschiedenartig und entspricht dem Kreis der stets wiederkehrenden Festtage. Am Anfang des Jahres werden die zahlreichen Karnevalfeste gefeiert, die am Sonnabend vor Fastnacht beginnen und bis zum Rosensonntag dauern. Zu den ty-

Citons ainsi parmi tant d'autres : le Rosenmontag d'Eupen et la danse obsédante et rythmée des Gilles de Binche qui sont 500; le chatoyant carnaval de Malmédy; le Tonnekensbrand de Grammont; la fête des chats d'Ypres; la grande fête carnavalesque d'Alost et le cortège des Chinels de Fosses; la grande liesse des Blancs Moussis de Stavelot et la cavalcade du Laetare de La Louvière.

Dès le dimanche des Rameaux ont lieu les premières processions de l'année qui se multiplieront jusqu'au déclin de l'été. Parmi les processions les plus célèbres, relevons la chevauchée d'Hakendover, la fameuse procession du Saint-Sang à Bruges, celle du Car d'Or à Mons, celle particulièrement pathétique des Pénitents à Furnes et celle dite de la Peste à Tournai.

Certaines de ces processions ressemblent étrangement à des cavalcades carnavalesques telles les Marches d'Entre-Sambre-et-Meuse avec leurs escortes de soldats de fantaisie, telles aussi celles de Lembecq et du « Fiertel » de Renaix. D'autres processions, sont des chevauchées nocturnes cependant que d'aucunes participent des ferveurs marines en se terminant par la bénédiction de la mer, tandis que d'autres encore, en Ardenne, précèdent une bénédiction de la forêt.

Avec les kermesses et les ducasses, nous assistons à la sortie des géants et à celle du cheval Bayard, à Ath pour ceux-ci, à Termonde et Bruxelles pour celui-là. En ce domaine, les villes wallonnes concurrencent en pittoresque leurs sœurs flamandes.

A l'automne, de nouvelles processions s'annoncent, mais ce sont à présent des processions aux chandelles, telle la grande procession de Montaigu. La Saint-Hubert appelle la bénédiction des meutes tandis que quelques jours plus tard à la Saint-Martin, commencent les fêtes de fin d'année en l'honneur des enfants, et ici le bon saint Martin, dans certaines villes flamandes tout au moins, entre en lice avec saint Nicolas et le Père Noël, tous trois rivalisant en générosité. Entre-temps les fêtes corporatives se sont également mises de la partie. Après sainte Cécile, patronne des musiciens, nous avons saint Éloi, patron des métallurgistes et sainte Barbe, patronne des mineurs, des pompiers et des artilleurs, pour ne citer que trois saints particulièrement honorés Mais nous allions oublier sainte Catherine, patronne des jeunes filles demeurées célibataires, et saint Aubert, patron des boulangers. Tous ces saints patrons ne sont évi-

behoren de Rosenmontag te Eupen, de ritmische en meeslepende dansen van de vijfhonderd Gilles te Binche, het kleurige karnaval te Malmedy, de Tonnekensbrand te Geeraardsbergen en het Kattenfeest te Ieper; de grote karnavaloptocht te Aalst, de stoet der 'Chinnels' te Fosses; de grote kermis van de 'Blancs Moussis' te Stavelot en de Laetarekavalkade te La Louvière.

Op Palmzondag grijpen de eerste processies van het jaar plaats. Ze volgen elkaar op tot het einde van de zomer. Tot de meest beroemde behoren de paardenprocessie te Hakendover, de H. Bloedprocessie te Brugge, die van de 'Car d'Or' te Bergen, de bijzonder aangrijpende Boetprocessie te Veurne en de zgn. 'pestprocessie' te Doornik.

Sommige dezer processies vertonen grote gelijkenis met de karnavalstoeten. Dit geldt voor de 'Marches d'Entre-Sambre-et-Meuse', met hun escorten van fantasiesoldaten, voor die van Lembeek en de van de 'Fiertel' te Ronse. Zekere processies zijn nachtelijke kavalkaden of worden besloten met de zegening van de zee, en in de Ardennen met die van de bossen.

Naast de kermissen noemen we de optocht van de reuzen te Aat en die van het Ros Beiaard te Dendermonde, waarbij de Waalse met de Vlaamse steden schijnen te wedijveren op het gebied van het typisch volkse.

In het najaar komen andere processies aan de beurt, zoals b.v. de Kaarskensprocessie te Scherpenheuvel. Op Sint-Hubertusdag worde jachthonden gezegend, terwijl enkele dagen later, op Sint-Martinus de oudejaarsfeesten voor de kinderen beginnen, in sommige Vlaamse steden wedijvert de goede Sint-Martinus met Sint-Niklaas en het Kerstmannetje in vrijgevigheid voor de kinderen. Veel afwisseling kenschetst de gildevieringen. Na Sint-Cecilia, de patrones van de muzikanten, zijn het Sint-Elooi, de patroon van de metaalbewerkers en Sint-Barbara, de patrones van de mijnwerkers, de brandweer en de artillerie, die de grootste verering genieten. Laten we de H. Catharina de patrones van de ongehuwde meisjes en de H. Aubertus, de patroon van de bakkers niet vergeten. Wel behoren deze beschermheiligen niet tot het specifiek Belgisch heiligenpatrimonium, maar zowel in de Vlaamse als in de Waalse provinciën zijn zij het voorwerp van specifiek Belgische volksgebruiken.

Op Kerst- en Oudejaarsavond, tijdens familiefeestjes en réveillons, kan het Belgische volk zijn drang

montag; the obsessive, rhythmical dancing of the 500 Gilles at Binche; Malmedy's colourful carnival; Geraardsbergen's Tonnekens brand; the celebration of the cats, at Ieperen; the great carnival festivities at Aalst, and the Chinels' procession at Fosses; the gaieties of the Blancs Moussis at Stavelot, and the Laetare cavalcade at La Louvière.

On Palm Sunday the year's first processions are being held; they will multiply until the close of the Summer. Among the most famous processions we should note the cavalcade at Hakendover, the celebrated procession of the Holy Blood in Brugge, the Car d'Or in Mons, the moving procession of the Penitents in Veurne, and the procession of the Plague in Tournai.

Some of these processions are more like carnival cavalcades: the "Marches d'Entre-Sambre-et-Meuse", with their escort of comedy soldiers, the Lembecq parade, and the "Fiertel" at Ronse.

Other processions take the form of nocturnal rides, or end with a benediction of the sea, or again, in the Ardennes, culminate in the blessing of the forest.

Fairs and patronal feasts are marked by the appearance of giants—i.a. at Ath—or the Bayard horse, in Dendermonde. In this respect the Walloon cities vie with the Flemish towns in producing spectacular shows.

Other processions are scheduled for the Autumn, but these are different in character, as illustrated by the big candle procession at Scherpenheuvel. On St.Hubert's day, the packs of hunting hounds are blessed, and a few days later, St. Martin's day marks the beginnings of the end-of-the-year festive occasions for the children. In some of the flemish towns St. Martin competes with St. Nicholas and Father Christmas in generosity towards the very young. Meanwhile, the season is also marked by guild celebrations. After St. Cecilia, patron saint of the musicians, St. Eligius is commemorated by the metal-workers, St. Barbara by the mine-workers, the firemen and the gunners, to quote only the most popular patron saints. We should also mention St. Catherine, protector of the unmarried girls, and St. Aubert, patron saint of the bakers. These patron saints, of course, are not confined to Belgium, but in both the Walloon and Flemish provinces they have produced, over the centuries, specific local customs.

Then come Christmas and new-year's eve, with their family cele-

pischen gehören der Rosenmontag zu Eupen, die rhythmischen und mitreissenden Tänze der fünfhundert Gilles zu Binche, der farbenfrohe Karneval zu Malmédy, der »Tonnekensbrand« zu Geraardsbergen und das Katzenfest zu Ieper, der grosse Karnevalsaufzug zu Aalst, der Aufzug der »Chinnels« zu Fosses, die grosse Kirmes der »Blancs Moussis« zu Stavelot und die Laetare-Kavalkade in La Louvière.

Am Palmsonntag beginnen die ersten Prozessionen des Jahres, die aufeinander folgen bis zum Ende des Sommers. Zu den berühmtesten gehören die Pferdprozession zu Hakendover und die Blutprozession zu Brügge, die des »Car d'Or« zu Mons, die besonders eindrucksvolle und angreifende Bussprozession zu Veurne und die zu Tournai, letztere bekannt als »Pestprozession«.

Manche dieser Prozessionen gleichen mehr einem Karnevalsaufzug. Das ist der Fall bei den »Marches d'Entre-Sambre-et-Meuse« mit ihren Eskorten von Fantasiesoldaten; auch die Prozessionen von Lembeek und Ronse, »Fiertel« genannt, haben das Karnevaleske.

Verschiedene Prozessionen sind nächtliche Kavalkaden oder endigen mit einer Seesegnung oder, wie in den Ardennen, mit der Segnung der Wälder.

Daneben gibt es noch den Aufzug der Riesen von Ath und den des Rosses Beiaard zu Dendermonde. Bei diesen Festen scheinen die wallonischen und flämischen Städte zu wetteifern, um dat Typischste und Volkstümlichste zu bringen.

Im Herbst kommen andere Prozessionen an die Reihe, so z.B. die Kerzenprozession zu Scherpenheuvel. Am St Hubertustag werden die Jagdhunde gesegnet, und einige Tage später, am St Martinstag, beginnen die Jahreswendefeste der Kinder. In verschiedenen flämischen Städten wetteifert der gute St Martin mit dem St Nikolaus und dem Weihnachtsmann durch Freigebigkeit gegenüber den Kindern. Viel Abwechslung kennzeichnet die Zunftfeste. Nach St Cecilia, der Schutzheiligen der Musik, ist es St Elooi, der Schutzheilige der Metallarbeiter, und St Barbara, die Schutzheilige der Bergarbeiter, der Feuerwehr und der Artillerie. Aber wir dürfen die Hl. Catharina, die Beschützerin der ledigen Mädchen, und den Hl. Aubertus, Patron der Bäcker, nicht vergessen. Diese Heiligen gehören natürlich nicht allein den Belgiern, aber in den flämischen wie auch den wallonischen Provinzen sind sie der Anlass von besonderen Volksgebräuchen.

Anlässlich von Weihnachts- und

demment pas propres à la Belgique seule, ce qui n'empêche que dans les provinces tant flamandes que wallonnes ils sont l'objet de coutumes folkloriques exclusivement belges. Enfin, ce sont la Noël et la Saint-Sylvestre avec leurs joies familiales et leurs réveillons au cours desquels le peuple belge a amplement l'occasion de déployer son goût du luxe et de la bonne chère.

Au cours de l'année, la jeunesse a également connu nombre de goûters matrimoniaux tantôt offerts aux jeunes gens, par les filles à marier comme à Écaussines, tantôt par les célibataires aux jeunes filles.

Vers la fin de l'année, y répondent les marchés aux fiançailles et autres fêtes de la jeunesse, notamment à Bastogne et à Arlon, qui ne sont que prétextes à danceries.

En toutes ces fêtes et manifestations du folklore belge se retrouvent des traditions qui remontent souvent au moyen âge et qui nous prouvent à quel point le peuple belge, cependant si féru de progrès et de modernisme, demeure profondément attaché à son glorieux passé.

Bien que carillons et béguinages ne relèvent point à proprement parler du folklore, il convient certainement d'évoquer ici ces deux aspects à la fois si émouvants et si beaux de l'esprit traditionnaliste du peuple belge. La musique du carillon qui s'égrène des tours des beffrois ou des églises, tant en pays flamand qu'en terre wallonne, a depuis toujours enchanté l'oreille de ceux qui visitent les villes d'art belges. Nous ne citerons ici que le plus célèbre de ces carillons, celui de la cathédrale Saint-Rombaut de Malines, la ville archiépiscopale qui recèle également en ses murs une école de carillon.

Et que dire des béguinages, ces oasis de paix et de recueillement, où le cours du temps semble s'être arrêté en plein moyen âge? Il faut les avoir visités pour comprendre pleinement l'âme belge et plus particulièrement l'art des Primitifs flamands. Les plus célèbres et les plus grands de ces béguinages sont ceux de Bruges, Gand, Louvain, Diest et Lierre.

naar vertier volledig uitleven en uitbundig pret maken.

Het hele jaar door richt de jeugd gezellige partijtjes in, waar ofwel de huwbare meisjes de jongens uitnodigen, zoals te Ecaussines, ofwel omgekeerd.

Tegen het einde van het jaar hebben, te Bastenaken en te Aarlen, de verlovingsmarkten plaats, naast andere feesten voor de jeugd, die ten slotte niets anders zijn dan gezellige danspartijtjes.

De vroomheid wordt in de Belgische folklore veruiterlijkt door talrijke bedevaarten, waarvan sommige eer profane manifestaties zijn geworden, terwijl andere gekenmerkt blijven door een mystieke ernst, die zelfs op niet-gelovigen diepe indruk maakt.

Het uitgangspunt van al deze feestelijkheden en uitingen van de Belgische folklore vormen traditites, die soms tot de Middeleeuwen teruggaan en het bewijs leveren dat het Belgische volk, hoe vooruitstrevend en modernistisch het ook voelt, sterk gehecht blijft aan zijn glorierijk verleden.

Hoewel klokkenspellen en begijnhoven niet tot het domein van de folklore behoren, past het te wijzen op deze twee zo ontroerende als typische aspecten van de traditionalistische geest van het Belgische volk. De beiaardklanken, die van de torens van belforten of kerken druppelen zowel in Vlaanderen als in Wallonië, hebben steeds de bezoekers der Belgische kunststeden bekoord. Het beroemdste van al deze klokkenspelen is dat van de Sint-Romboutskathedraal te Mechelen, de aartsbisschoppelijke stad, die er trots op is de enige beiaardierschool ter wereld te bezitten.

En welk een bekoring gaat niet uit van de begijnhoven, deze oasen van vrede en ingetogenheid, waar men zich in volle Middeleeuwen zou kunnen wanen. Men moet ze bezocht hebben om de Belgische ziel en meer bepaald de kunst van de Vlaamse Primitieven te begrijpen. De meest beroemde en de grootste zijn die van Brugge, Gent, Leuven, Diest en Lier.

brations and midnight suppers, during which the Belgian population can indulge in ostentation and good food.

During the year, the younger generation has taken part in a number of matrimonial afternoon meals, whether organised by girls of a marrying age for young men, as at Ecaussines, or by young bachelors for girls.

This leads, towards the end of the year, to engagement markets and other youthful celebrations, e.g. at Bastogne and Arlon, which are essentially local feasts with dancing.

On the level of devotion, the Belgian folk-lore features a number of pilgrimages, some of which are rather ungodly, while others display a truly mystical fervour that even agnostics find impressive.

All these celebrations and events in Belgian folk-lore keep alive traditions, many of which go back to the Middle Ages. They demonstrate the population's profound attachment to its past, despite its eagerness for progress and innovation.

Carillons and beguine convents, although not belonging to folk-lore, deserve to be mentioned as two beautiful and outstanding features of the great Belgian tradition. The chiming of the bells in church spires or belfries, both in the Flemish area and the Walloon region, gives a special character to the experience of the visiting tourist. The most famous carillon in the country is in the tower of St. Rombouts' cathedral at Mechelen, the archi-episcopal seat, and the only city in the world where there is a carillon school.

As to the beguine convents, they are unique abodes of peace and meditation, where time seems to have stopped since the Middle Ages. More than anything else, they throw light on the Belgian soul, particularly on the works of Flemish primitive painting. The largest and most famous beguine convents are at Brugge and Ghent. The one at Anderlencht, a suburb of Brussels, is the smallest one in the country.

Sylvesterfeiern, auf Familien- und anderen Festen kann der Belgier sich völlig der Freude und dem Spass überlassen.

Das ganze Jahr durch gibt die Jugend Parties, wo z.B. die heiratslustigen Mädchen die Jungens einladen, wie es in Ecaussines gebräuchlich ist.

Gegen Ende des Jahres finden in Bastogne und Arlon die Verlobungsmärkte statt, die schliesslich nichts anderes als fröhliche Tanzfeste sind.

Die Frömmigkeit kommt in der belgischen Folklore in den zahlreichen Wallfahrten zum Ausdruck. Einige davon sind indessen schon beinahe weltliche Veranstaltungen geworden, während andere den mystischen Ernst behalten haben, der selbst auf Nichtgläubige tiefen Eindruck macht.

Alle diese Feste und Feiern stammen aus der Tradition, die manchmal bis ins Mittelalter zurückreicht. Sie beweisen, dass das belgische Volk, so fortgeschrittlich und modern es auch ist, stark an die Vergangenheit gebunden ist.

Obwohl Glockenspiele und Beginenhöfe nicht zur eigentlichen Folklore gehören, passt es doch, auf diese ebenso ergreifenden wie typischen Aspekte des traditionsgebundenen Geistes der Belgier hinzuweisen. Die Glockenspielklänge, die von den Türmen der Belfriede oder Kirchen ertönen, so in Flandern wie in Wallonien haben stets die Besucher entzückt. Das berühmteste dieser Glockenspiele ist das der Romboutskathedrale zu Mechelen, der erzbischöflichen Stadt, die stolz darauf ist, die einzige Glockenspielerschule der Welt zu besitzen.

Und welch wohltätige Ruhe, welch ein Zauber geht nicht von den Beginenhöfen aus, diesen Oasen von Frieden und Besinnung, wo man sich noch im Mittelalter wähnen könnte. Man muss sie besucht haben, um die belgische Seele und noch mehr die Kunst der flämischen Primitiven zu begreifen. Die berühmtesten Beginenhöfe sind die von Brügge, Gent, Löwen, Diest und Lier.

L'HISTOIRE

Comme le prouvent les nombreuses découvertes faites dans le sous-sol de la Belgique, le pays était peuplé, dès la période paléolithique, par des hommes particulièrement industrieux qui vivaient surtout de la pêche et de la chasse.

Au cours de l'âge du bronze, les Celtes établirent leur hégémonie sur

DE GESCHIEDENIS

Zoals blijkt uit talrijke opgravingen, was het land reeds bevolkt in het paleolithische tijdvak door mensen die zeer bedrijvig waren, en die hoofdzakelijk leefden van jacht en visvangst.

In het bronstijdperk vestigden de Kelten hun hegemonie over het land, maar weldra verschenen ook

BELGIAN HISTORY

Numerous discoveries in the Belgian subsoil have indicated that the country, in the paleolithic era, had a highly industrious population, whose main resources were fishing and hunting.

During the bronze age the Celts conquered the country. They soon

DIE GESCHICHTE

Wie man aus den zahlreichen Ausgrabungen schliessen kann, war das Land bereits im Paläolithikum durch Menschen, die vor allem von Jagd und Fischfang lebten, bewohnt.

In der Bronzezeit festigten die Kelten hier ihre Oberherrschaft. Bald aber kamen auch die Belgier, die wahrscheinlich germanischen

le pays, bientôt rejoints par les Belges, vraisemblablement d'origine germanique.

Puis ce fut la conquête par les légions de Jules César, suivie de la première période historique qui fut une ère de prospérité sous l'égide de la Pax Romana. C'est à cette époque que le christianisme fit également son apparition dans la Gaule belge sans toutefois pouvoir s'y implanter profondément.

Les invasions franques du Ve siècle mirent brutalement fin à la prospérité romaine, sans toutefois parvenir à effacer complètement les traces de quatre siècles de civilisation.

Après quelques lustres de désarroi complet, les provinces belges reprirent au cours du Ve siècle leur lente ascencion vers des temps meilleurs.

Cette ascension fut amorcée par le roi mérovingien Childéric et accélérée par son fils Clovis (466-511) qui se convertit au christianisme et étendit le royaume franc jusque fort avant dans le territoire de la France actuelle.

A son décès, le royaume franc fut partagé entre ses fils, puis à nouveau unifié sous le règne de Clotaire I († 561). Les fils de celui-ci partagèrent à leur tour l'héritage royal en deux royaumes mérovingiens : la Neustrie et l'Austrasie. Sous Dagobert († 639), il y eut une ultime unification, puis ce fut la décadence de la dynastie mérovingienne, dont les derniers descendants furent appelés les « rois fainéants ».

La famille austrasienne des Pépinides prit leur succession, refaisant de l'Austrasie (la région entre Meuse, Rhin et Moselle) le centre de gravité du royaume franc. Les deux plus illustres représentants de cette famille sont Charles Martel, le vainqueur des Sarrasins à Poitiers (732), et Charlemagne (742-814) du nom desquels cette dynastie prit le nom de dynastie carolingienne.

Charlemagne fut un grand conquérant et un non moins grand unificateur de terres, aussi devint-il en 800 empereur d'Occident. Son empire s'étendait depuis l'Atlantique et la mer du Nord jusqu'au centre de l'Europe d'une part et jusqu'à la Méditerranée de l'autre.

Cet empire immense, qui était comme la réincarnation de l'empire romain, fut morcelé à son tour par le Traité de Verdun (843), cette fois en trois royaumes : la Francia Occidentalis, la Francia Media et la Francia Orientalis. La Belgique actuelle fut scindée à cette occasion en deux, avec le cours de l'Escaut comme frontière entre les deux : à l'ouest du fleuve le territoire fut

de Belgen die waarschijnlijk van Germaanse oorsprong waren.

Toen volgde de verovering door de legioenen van Julius Cesar, die een tijdvak van grote voorspoed onder de Pax Romana inluidde. Het is in die tijd dat het Christendom zijn intrede deed in Belgisch Gallië, zonder er nochtans diep wortel te schieten.

De Frankische invallen van de 5de eeuw maakten op gewelddadige wijze een einde aan de Romeinse voorspoed, zonder evenwel de sporen van vier eeuwen beschaving volledig uit te wissen.

Na enkele tientallen jaren van volkomen ontreddering begonnen de Belgische provinciën in de loop van de 5de eeuw hun geleidelijke opgang naar betere tijden.

Deze opgang werd ingeluid door de Merovingische koning Childerik, en bespoedigd door zijn zoon Clovis (466-511), die zich tot het Christendom bekeerde, en het jonge Frankische rijk uitbreidde tot ver op het grondgebied van het huidige Frankrijk.

Na zijn dood werd het Frankische rijk verdeeld onder zijn zonen en vervolgens opnieuw verenigd onder de regering van Lotharius I († 561). Zijn zonen verdeelden op hun beurt hun koninklijke erfenis in twee Merovingische rijken : dat van Neustrië en dat van Austrasië. Onder koning Dagobert († 639) kwam het tot een laatste eenmaking, gevolgd door het langzame verval van de Merovingische dynastie, waarvan de laatste afstammelingen in de geschiedenis bekend zijn als de 'vadsige koningen'.

De Austrasische familie der Pepijns trok alle macht naar zich toe, en maakte van Austrasië (de streek tussen Maas, Rijn en Moezel) opnieuw het zwaartepunt van het Frankische rijk. De twee beroemdste vertegenwoordigers van deze familie zijn Karel Martel, de overwinnaar der Saracenen te Poitiers (732) en Karel de Grote, die zijn naam gaf aan het Karolingische vorstenhuis.

Karel de Grote was een groot veroveraar en een niet minder groot gebiedsuitbreider, en zo werd hij in 800 tot Keizer van het Westen gekroond. Zijn keizerrijk strekte zich uit van de Atlantische Oceaan en de Noordzee tot in het hartje van Europa enerzijds en tot aan de Middellandse Zee anderzijds.

Dit onmetelijke keizerrijk, dat zowat een herrezen Romeins rijk was, werd op zijn beurt verbrokkeld door het Verdrag van Verdun (843), maar ditmaal in drie koninkrijken : Francia Occidentalis, Francia Media en Francia Orientalis. Het huidige

were joined by the Belgians, who probably were of German origin.

There followed the conquest by Julius Caesar's legions, which marked the beginnings of the country's history,—a period of prosperity, under the aegis of the Pax Romana. At that time Christianism also reached Belgian Gaul, but did not take root in the area.

Invasions by the Franks, in the 5th century, brought Roman prosperity to an abrupt end, but they did not entirely erase the marks of four centuries of civilization.

After some years of utter disarray, the Belgian provinces slowly began to recuperate, in the course of the 5th century.

The improvement was initiated by the Merovingian king Childeric, and accelerated by the latter's son Clovis (466-511), a convert to catholicism, who extended his Frankish kingdom into the present territory of France.

On his death, the Kingdom was apportioned between his sons, and again united under Clotar I († 561). His sons, in their turn, split the royal heritage in two Merovingian kingdoms: Neustria and Austrasia. Under Dagobert († 639), the country again was united, for the last time. Then, the decadence of the Merovingian dynasty set in: its last descendants were called "the sluggard Kings".

The Austrasian family of the Pepinides took over, making Austrasia (the area between Meuse, Rhine and Moselle) the centre of the Frankish kingdom. The family's most illustrious representatives are Charles Martel, who defeated the Saracens at Poitiers (732) and Charlemagne (742-814) who gave the dynasty its name.

Charlemagne was successful both in his conquests and in the unification of territories. In 800, he was created Emperor of the West. His Empire reached out from the Atlantic Ocean and the North Sea to the centre of Europe on the one hand, and the Mediterranean area on the other.

This huge Empire, a sort of remake of the Roman Empire, was broken up, in its turn, by the Treaty of Verdun (843), this time in three Kingdoms: Francia Occidentalis, Francia Media and Francia Orientalis. The Belgium of today,

Ursprungs waren. Dann folgte die Eroberung durch die Legionen Caesars, womit durch die Pax Romana eine Periode grosser Wohlfahrt begann. In dieser Zeit kam das Christentum nach belgisch Gallien, doch ohne tief Wurzel zu schlagen.

Der Einfall der Franken im 5. Jahrhundert beendigte auf gewaltsame Weise die römische Wohlfahrt, doch konnte er die Spuren der 400-jährigen Zivilisation nicht zu nichte machen. Nach einigen Jahren völliger Zerrüttung begann für die belgische Provinzen im Laufe des 5. Jahrhunderts ein langsamer Aufstieg zu besseren Zeiten.

Dieser Aufstieg begann mit der Herrschaft des merovingischen Königs Childerich und wurde beschleunigt durch seinen Sohn Chlodwig (466-511), der sich zum Christentum bekehrte und das junge Fränkische Reich bis weit auf das heutige Grundgebiet Frankreichs ausbreitete. Nach seinem Tode wurde das Fränkische Reich geteilt zwischen seinen Söhnen und später wieder vereinigt unter der Regierung von Lothar I. († 561). Dessen Söhne wiederum teilten ihr königliches Erbe in zwei merovingische Reiche: Neustrien und Austrasien. Nachdem das Reich zum letzten Male unter Dagobert († 639) vereinigt war, folgte ein langsamer Verfall der merovingischen Dynastie, deren letzte Nachfahren in die Geschichte eingegangen sind als die »faulen« Könige.

Die austrasische Familie der Pippins riss alle Macht an sich und machte aus Austrasien (die Strecke zwischen Maas, Rhein und Mosel) aufs neue den Mittelpunkt des Fränkischen Reiches. Die zwei berühmtesten Vertreter dieser Familie sind Karl Martell, der Sieger über die Sarazenen bei Poitiers (732), und Karl der Grosse, der seinen Nahmen an das Karolingische Fürstenhaus gab.

Karl der Grosse war ein unbesiegbarer Eroberer und ein grosser Mehrer seines Reiches. So wurde er 800 zum Kaiser des Westens gekrönt. Sein Kaiserreich erstreckte sich vom Atlantischen Ozean und der Nordsee bis in das Herz Europas und bis an das Mittelmeer aus. Dieses unermessliche Kaiserreich, das ungefähr das neuerstandene Römische Reich war, wurde zerstückelt durch den Vertrag von Verdun (843), doch diesmal in drei Königreiche : Francia Occidentalis, Francia Media, Francia Orientalis. Das heutige Belgien wurde geteilt, mit der Schelde als Grenze zwischen beiden Gebieten : das Stück westlich der Schelde fiel Karl dem

dévolu à Charles le Chauve et à l'est (la Lotharingie) à Lothaire II. Cette frontière subsista, féodalement tout au moins, jusqu'au milieu du XVIe siècle et ne fut abolie que par la Pragmatique Sanction d'Augsbourg (1549).

Au cours du IXe siècle, au lendemain et à l'occasion même de nouvelles invasions, surtout normandes, tant terrestres que maritimes, s'amorça la période féodale. Les bases du futur comté de Flandre furent alors établies par Baudouin Ier Bras de Fer.

De leur côté le duché de Brabant, la principauté de Liège, le comté du Hainaut, le comté de Namur, ainsi que plusieurs petits états féodaux, prirent alors naissance sur le territoire de ce qui allait devenir la Belgique. Le rêve constant des grands féodaux belges fut dès lors de réunir tous ces petits états sous un seul sceptre, rêve que parvinrent enfin à réaliser, au cours du XVe siècle, les ducs de Bourgogne. Entre-temps, l'histoire de Belgique fut une longue suite de remous féodaux : guerres entre états avec annexions de territoires soit par la force, soit par la voie des alliances; guerre entre vassaux et suzerains; guerres entre communes etc.

Notons ici deux grandes dates : la Bataille de Woeringen (1288), où le duc de Brabant Jean Ier remporta la victoire, ce qui lui permit d'annexer le Limbourg; la Bataille des Éperons d'Or (1302), où les communiers flamands battirent la fleur de la noblesse française, assurant ainsi définitivement l'indépendance des provinces flamandes vis-à-vis de la France.

A la fin du XIe siècle, eut lieu la première Croisade avec Godefroid de Bouillon et Robert II, comte de Flandre, comme grands chefs militaires. Les comtes de Flandre Thierry et Philippe d'Alsace, eux, se distinguèrent respectivement à la deuxième et à la troisième Croisade.

Sur le plan économique et social, l'époque féodale fut également pleine d'événements capitaux pour l'histoire du pays. C'est à cette époque, en effet, que celui-ci vit naître la plupart de ses villes et de ses villages, ainsi que de nombreuses abbayes, toutes grandes défricheuses de bois et de terres incultes. Les moines jouèrent, en outre, un rôle capital dans l'éducation du peuple.

Le commerce s'organisa et d'importantes industries dont l'industrie textile, se développèrent dans des villes de plus en plus prospères dont les habitants surent conquérir des franchises de plus en plus libérales. C'est l'origine du système commu-

België werd in twee gesneden, met de loop van de Schelde als grens tussen de beide delen : het stuk dat ten westen van deze stroom is gelegen viel ten deel aan Karel de Kale, terwijl het oostelijk gedeelte (Lotharingen) aan Lotharius II werd geschonken.

De aanvang van het leenroerig tijdperk klimt op tot de 9de eeuw, na en als gevolg van nieuwe invallen, zowel te land als vanuit de zee, vooral van de Noormannen. Toen legde Boudewijn I, met de IJzeren Arm, de grondslagen van het toekomstige graafschap Vlaanderen.

In die tijd ontstonden tevens het hertogdom Brabant, het prinsbisdom Luik, het graafschap Henegouwen, het graafschap Namen en nog verscheidene kleine feodale staatjes op het grondgebied, dat later België zou worden. Het was de voortdurende droom van de grote Belgische adellijke heersers, al deze kleine, afzonderlijke staatjes onder één enkele scepter te verenigen, en tenslotte zouden de hertogen van Bourgondië er in de 15de eeuw in slagen, die droom te verwezenlijken. Maar vóór het zo ver is, biedt de geschiedenis van België één lange opvolging van feodale beroeringen : oorlogen onder de verschillende staten, gebiedsnaasting met geweld of door middel van huwelijken; oorlogen tussen vazallen en suzereinen, strijd tussen de gemeenten, enz.

Hier zijn twee grote data te vermelden : de Slag van Woeringen (1288), waar de hertog van Brabant, Jan I, de Overwinnaar, het pleit won, en waardoor het hem mogelijk werd Limburg bij Brabant te voegen, en de Slag der Gulden Sporen (1302) waar de Vlaamse gemeentenaren het puik van de Franse ridderschap onder de voet liepen.

Op het einde van de 11de eeuw grijpt de eerste Kruistocht plaats, met Godfried van Bouillon en Robrecht II van Vlaanderen als grote militaire leiders. De graven van Vlaanderen, Diederik en Filips van de Elzas, onderscheidden zich respectievelijk in de tweede en de derde kruistocht.

Op economisch en sociaal gebied was het leenroerig tijdvak gekenmerkt door gewichtige historische gebeurtenissen. De meeste steden en dorpen ontstaan, talrijke abdijen worden gesticht die zich toeleggen op het ontginnen van bossen en braakliggende gronden. De monniken speelden bovendien een belangrijke rol in de opvoeding van het volk.

De handel werd georganiseerd en belangrijke nijverheidstakken, zoals de textielindustrie kwamen tot ont-

on this occasion, was split up in two parts, with the course of the Scheldt as common frontier: the territoiries West of the river were given to Charles the Bald, and the Eastern area (Lotharingia), to Lothar II. The frontier remained in existence, at least in terms of feudalism, until the middle of the 16th century, when it was abolished at Augsburg by the Pragmatic Sanction (1549).

New invasions—mainly by Normans, who came both by land and sea—marked the beginning of the feudal era. Baldwin Bras de Fer laid the grounds of the future County of Flanders.

On the other side, the Duchy of Brabant, the Principality of Liège, the Countries of Hainaut and Namur, together with several smaller feudal states, were created in the area that would be Belgium several centuries later. The great feudal lords' constant ambition was to unite all these small states under a single monarch. The Dukes of Burgundy were to make the dream come true, in the course of the 15th century.

In the meantime, the history of Belgium was one long succession of feudal upheavals: wars between states, and territorial expansion either by force or by marriage; wars between vassals and suzerain lord; wars between towns, etc...

We will note two main dates: the Battle at Woeringen (1288), won by Jean I, Duke of Brabant, enabling him to annex Limburg; the Battle of the Golden Spurs (1302), in which the Flemish militia defeated the elite of French aristocracy, thereby establishing the lasting independence of the Flemish provinces vis-à-vis France.

The first Crusade—with Godefroid de Bouillon and Robert II, count of Flanders, as military leaders—took place at the end of the 11th century. Thierry and Philippe d'Alsace, counts of Flanders, were to distinguish themselves, respectively in the second and third Crusade.

The feudal era was also full of decisive events for the history of the country, in the economic and social fields. In those days, most cities and villages were created; many abbeys came into being, and this accelerated the reclamation of forests and uncultivated land. The monks, moreover, played a decisive role in the education of the people.

Kahlen zu, während der östliche Teil (Lothringen) dem Lothar II. geschenkt wurde. Diese Grenzlinie blieb, wenigstens feudal gesehen, bestehen bis Mitte des 16. Jahrhunderts und wurde erst mit der Pragmatischen Sanktion von Augsburg (1549) abgeschafft.

Der Anfang des Lehnswesens reicht zurück bis in das 9. Jahrhundert. Es entstand durch die Einfälle der Normannen zu Wasser und zu Lande. Damals legte Balduin mit dem Eisernen Arm die Grundlagen der zukünftigen Grafschaft Flandern.

In dieser Zeit entstanden auch auf dem Grundgebiet des späteren Belgiens das Herzogtum Brabant, das Fürstbistum Lüttich, die Grafschaft Hainaut, die Grafschaft Namur und noch verschiedene andere sehr kleine feudale Staaten. Es war der Traum der grossen belgischen Herrscher alle diese kleinen abgesonderten Staaten unter einem Zepter zu vereinigen. Schliesslich gelang es den Herzögen von Burgund im 15. Jahrhundert diesen Traum zu verwirklichen. Aber bevor es so weit war, zeigt die Geschichte Belgiens eine lange Reihe feudaler Aufstände, Kriege zwischen den verschiedenen Staaten, Gebietsveränderungen durch Gewalt oder Heirat, Kriege zwischen Vasallen und Suzeräne, Streitigkeiten zwischen den Gemeinden, usw.

Hier sind zwei wichtige Daten zu erwähnen : die Schlacht bei Woeringen (1288), wo Johan I. (der Sieger) von Brabant, den Streit gewann und wodurch es ihm möglich wurde Limburg zu Brabant zu fügen; und die Goldene-Sporen-Schlacht (1302) wo die flämischen Bürger die Blüte der französischen Ritterschaft bei Kortrijk vernichteten.

Unter Gottfried von Bouillon und Robrecht II. von Flandern, den grossen militärischen Führern, begann gegen Ende des 11. Jahrhundert der erste Kreuzzug. Die Grafen von Flandern, Diederich und Philipp vom Elsass, zeichneten sich im 2. und 3. Kreuzzug besonders aus.

Auf wirtschaftlichem und sozialem Gebiet war die Lehnszeit gekennzeichnet durch wichtige historische Ereignisse : die meisten der jetzigen Städte und Dörfer enstanden damals, zahlreiche Abteien wurden gegründet, die sich auf die Urbarmachung von Wäldern und Brachland verlegten. Die Mönche spielten vor allem eine wichtige Rolle in der Erziehung des Volkes, der Handel wurde organisiert. Wichtige Industriezweige, wie die Tuchindustrie

nal, essentiellement démocratique, qui se trouve à la base de nos conceptions politiques modernes.

Si le monde féodal fut l'œuvre de la noblesse et du haut clergé, le monde communal, lui, naquit du génie organisateur du patriciat et de l'artisanat des villes féodales, ces deux classes de la société entrant d'ailleurs bien souvent en conflit pour la conquête et l'exercice du pouvoir communal. Rappelons ici le nom du grand tribun gantois Jacques van Artevelde (1287-1345).

Deux grands événements constitutionnels marquèrent le XIVe siècle : la Paix de Fexhe (1316) qui accorda d'appréciables avantages et libertés aux habitants de la principauté de Liège et la Charte de Joyeuse Entrée (1356), accordée à ceux du duché de Brabant. La vie intellectuelle, un moment menacée par les invasions du IXe siècle, reprit un nouvel essor, pour aboutir à l'épanouissement d'abord de l'art roman, ensuite de l'art gothique. Le pays se couvrit alors de monuments remarquables, tant religieux que civils et militaires, et tous les arts, tant dans le domaine plastique que musical ou littéraire se mirent à fleurir, d'abord dans la vallée mosane, ensuite dans la région scaldienne.

Les ducs de Bourgogne de la branche cadette des Valois de France s'introduisirent en Belgique par le mariage de Philippe le Hardi avec Marguerite de Maele, fille unique du comte de Flandre, Louis de Maele.

Par une politique dynastique à longue échéance les ducs de Bourgogne successifs : Philippe le Hardi (1342-1404), Jean sans Peur (1371-1419), Philippe le Bon (1396-1467) et Charles le Téméraire (1433-1477) parvinrent à réunir sous leur sceptre nombre de petits territoires féodaux, actuellement français, belges et hollandais pour former une véritable terre d'entre-deux rappelant assez bien la Lotharingie de la fin de l'époque carolingienne, dont les provinces belges devinrent bientôt le centre de gravité. Philippe le Bon fut le premier des princes belges à pratiquer une politique non plus féodale, mais résolument nationale et centralisatrice. Si le règne de ce duc fut long et prospère, celui de Charles le Téméraire (1467-1477) connut au contraire, les fortunes diverses pour se terminer par la mort tragique du duc à la bataille de Nancy. Sa fille Marie de Bourgogne (1457-1482) lui succéda dans des circonstances difficiles, mais au cours de son règne éphémère, elle fut efficacement soutenue par son mari, Maximilien d'Autriche, de la dynastie des Habsbourg. Celui-ci

wikkeling in de steden, die voortdurend welvarender werden, en waarvan de bewoners steeds meer vrijheden verwierven.

Terwijl de feodale wereld het werk was van de adel en van de hoge geestelijkheid, was het gemeentestelsel de vrucht van het organisatievernuft van de patriciërs en de ambachtslieden van de feodale steden, alhoewel deze standen vaak met elkaar in conflict kwamen voor de verovering en de uitoefening van de gemeentelijke macht. In verband daarmee moet hier de naam genoemd worden van de grote Gentse volksleider Jakob van Artevelde (1287-1345).

Twee grote constitutionele gebeurtenissen kenmerken de 14de eeuw : de Vrede van Fexhe (1316) waardoor wezenlijke voordelen en vrijheden werden verleend aan de burgers van het prinsbisdom Luik, en de Keure van de Blijde Inkomste (1356) die gelijkaardige privilegiën toekende aan de burgers van het hertogdom Brabant. Het intellectuele leven, dat een ogenblik bedreigd was door de invallen der Noormannen in de 9de eeuw, nam een nieuwe vlucht en gaf aanleiding tot de ontplooiing van de romaanse kunst eerst, van de gotische kunst daarna.

De hertogen van Bourgondië, van de jongste tak van het Huis van Valois, verschenen in België door het huwelijk van Filips de Stoute met Margaretha van Male, de enige dochter van de graaf van Vlaanderen Lodewijk van Male.

Door hun dynastiepolitiek op lange termijn zijn de achtereenvolgende hertogen van Bourgondië: Filips de Stoute (1342-1404), Jan Zonder Vrees (1371-1419), Filips de Goede (1396-1467) en Karel de Stoute (1433-1477), er in geslaagd onder hun scepter tal van kleine feodale lenen, waarvan het grondgebied thans deel uitmaakt van Frankrijk, België en Nederland, te verenigen tot een ware bufferstaat, die veel gelijkenis vertoonde met het Lotharingen van het einde van het Karolingische tijdvak, en waarvan de Belgische provinciën, weldra het zwaartepunt zouden uitmaken. Filips de Goede was de eerste Belgische prins die niet langer een feodale, maar wel een beslist nationale en centraliserende politiek voerde. De regering van deze hertog was lang en voorspoedig maar zijn zoon Karel de Stoute had met allerlei moeilijkheden te kampen, die tenslotte leidden tot zijn tragische dood tijdens de slag bij Nancy (1477). Zijn dochter Maria van Bourgondië (1457-1482) volgde hem op in

Trade got underway, and important industries—such as the textile industry—developed in ever increasingly prosperous cities, whose inhabitants obtained increasingly liberal franchises. This is the origin of the "communal" system,—an essentially democratic one— which forms the basis of our modern political concepts.

The feudal world was shaped by the aristocracy and the high clergy; the "communal" world, on the other hand, was the result of the inventiveness of the feudal cities', patricians and craftsmen. The latter two social classes often clashed over the exercice of "communal" authority, as exemplified by the great democratic leader in Ghent, Jacques van Artevelde (1274-1345).

Two main constitutional developments mark the 14th century: the Peace of Fexhe (1316), which granted substantial advantages and franchises to the inhabitants of the Principality of Liège; and the "Charte de Joyeuse Entrée", granted to the people of the Duchy of Brabant (1356). Cultural life, that had been endangered by the 9th century invasions, took a fresh start, and culminated first in romanesque and subsequently in gothic art. All over the country, religious, civilian and military monuments were built, and all the arts—painting, sculpture, music, literature—flourished, first in the Meuse valley and, somewhat later, in the Scheldt area.

The Dukes of Burgundy—of the younger branch of the French Valois—came to Belgium through the marriage of Philippe le Hardi to Marguerite de Maele, only daughter of Louis de Maele, count of Flanders.

In a long-term dynastic policy, the successive Dukes of Burgundy— Philippe le Hardi (1342-1404), Jean sans Peur (1371-1419), Philippe le Bon (1396-1467) and Charles le Téméraire (1433-1477) succeeded in establishing their authority over a number of feudal territories that now are French, Belgian and Dutch. Their Dukedom was a truly inbetween realm, recalling the Lotharingia of carlovingian days; the Belgian provinces formed its nucleus. Philippe le Bon was one of the first Belgian princes to replace feudal approaches by an outspoken national, centralistic policy.

His reign was long lasting and brought prosperity. His successor, however, Charles le Téméraire

entwickelten sich in den Städten. Dadurch wurden diese wohlhabender und die Stadtbewohner erwarben immer mehr Privilegien. Hier ist auch der Ursprung zu suchen des Gemeindesystems, eines ausserordentlich demokratischen Systems, das die Grundlage unserer modernen politischen Einstellung ist.

Während die Feudalwelt das Werk des Adels und der hohen Geistlichkeit war, war das Gemeindesystem die Frucht des Organisationstalentes der Patrizier und der Handwerker aus den feudalen Städten. Doch kamen die zwei Stände oftmals miteinander in Konflikt, wegen der Eroberung und Ausübung der kommunalen Macht. Im Zusammenhang hiermit erwähnen wir den grossen Volksführer aus Gent, Jacob van Artevelde (1274-1345).

Zwei grosse verfassungsmässige Ereignisse kennzeichnen das 14. Jahrhundert : der Friede von Fexhe (1316), wodurch den Bürgern des Fürstbistums Lüttich wesentliche Vorteile und Freiheiten verliehen wurden, und die »Keure van de blijde Inkomste« (1356), die gleichartige Privilegien den Bürgern des Herzogtums Brabant zuerkannten.

Das intellektuelle Leben, das zur Zeit der Einfälle der Normannen im 9. Jahrhundert gefährdet war, nahm einen neuen Aufschwung und gab Anregung zur Entfaltung der romanischen, später gotischen Kunst. Bemerkenswerte kirchliche, bürgerliche sowie militärische Bauwerke entstanden. Auch die bildenden Künste, wie auch die Musik und die Literatur entwickelten sich zu ungeahnten Höhen, zuerst im Maas-, dann im Scheldetal.

Die Herzöge von Burgund, Abkömmlinge des jüngsten Zweiges des Hauses Valois, kamen durch die Heirat Philipps des Kühnen mit Margarete von Male, einziger Tochter des Grafen von Flandern, Ludwig von Male, nach Belgien.

Durch Dynastiepolitik auf lange Frist ist es den aufeinanderfolgenden Herzögen von Burgund : Philipp dem Kühnen (1342-1404), Johan ohne Furcht (1371-1419), Philipp dem Guten (1396-1467) und Karl dem Kühnen (1433-1477) gelungen, unter ihrem Zepter eine grosse Anzahl kleiner feudaler Lehen zu vereinigen zu einem wahren Pufferstaat. Dieses Grundgebiet (jetzt ein Teil von Frankreich, nebst Belgien und Holland) hatte viel Ähnlichkeit mit dem Lothringen aus der Karolingerzeit. Die belgischen Provinzen waren bald der Schwerpunkt dieses Gebietes. Philipp der Gute war der erste belgische Fürst, der nicht

assura d'ailleurs la régence du duché, après la mort prématurée de sa femme, durant la minorité de leur fils, Philippe le Beau (1478-1506).

Le mariage de Marie de Bourgogne avec Maximilien d'Autriche eut comme conséquence de faire passer nos provinces sous la dépendance de souverains disposant de domaines beaucoup plus importants que le nôtre; ainsi, pendant plusieurs siècles, notre Gouvernement allait se borner à une autonomie locale plus ou moins grande, au sein d'empires très étendus qui retenaient davantage l'attention de nos princes. Le fils de Marie de Bourgogne et de Maximilien, Philippe le Beau épousa Jeanne de Castille, connue dans l'histoire sous le nom de Jeanne la Folle. Philippe devint, par sa femme, l'héritier de l'empire espagnol et monta sur le trône d'Espagne, en 1504, tout en conservant sur les Pays-Bas, la souveraineté qu'il exerçait personnellement depuis 1494.

Il mourut malheureusement deux ans plus tard. Son fils, Charles Quint (1500-1558), né à Gand, devint en 1515, souverain des Pays-Bas, en 1517, roi d'Espagne et en 1519, empereur d'Allemagne, cependant que par la Pragmatique Sanction de 1549, il fut le fondateur des XVII Provinces ou Cercle de Bourgogne, que Charles Quint voulait constituer en un « bloc indivisible et impartageable »; les provinces belges actuelles formaient la majeure partie méridionale du « Cercle ».

Durant le règne de Charles Quint la Renaissance fit sa triomphale entrée dans les Pays-Bas méridionaux, tandis que la première génération des humanistes belges se fit un des plus grands centres intellectuels et scientifiques de l'Occident. Cependant c'est sous son règne que le mouvement de Réforme, qui fut fatal pour l'unité du « Cercle de Bourgogne », commença à s'affirmer.

Si Charles Quint se considéra toujours comme un prince des Pays-Bas, en dépit de ses couronnes de roi d'Espagne et d'empereur d'Allemagne, son fils Philippe II (1527-1589), au contraire, ne fut plus qu'un monarque étranger régnant sur ses provinces belges depuis la lointaine Cour d'Espagne.

Il laissa le pouvoir effectif sur ses provinces du nord entre les mains de gouvernantes et de gouverneurs qui ne purent empêcher qu'une véritable guerre de religion ravageât les Pays-Bas tant matériellement que moralement. La paix une fois revenue, le « Cercle de Bourgogne » n'était plus qu'un souvenir et à sa place étaient nés d'une part les

buitengewoon moeilijke omstandigheden, maar tijdens haar kortstondige regering werd zij metterdaad gesteund door haar echtgenoot Maximiliaan van Oostenrijk, van de dynastie der Habsburgers. Na de vroegtijdige dood van zijn vrouw, nam hij het regentschap over het hertogdom waar, zolang hun zoon, Filips de Schone (1478-1506), nog minderjarig was.

Door het huwelijk van Maria van Bourgondië met Maximiliaan van Oostenrijk kwamen onze provinciën onder het gezag van vorsten die heersten over veel aanzienlijker gebieden; gedurende verscheidene eeuwen zou ons bestuur dan ook beperkt blijven tot een min of meer ruime plaatselijke autonomie in het verband van zeer uitgestrekte rijken, die al de waakzaamheid van onze prinsen kwamen opeisen. De zoon van Maria van Bourgondië en van Maximiliaan, Filips de Schone, trad in het huwelijk met Johanna van Castilië, in de geschiedenis bekend als Johanna de Krankzinnige. Door zijn vrouw werd Filips onverwacht de erfgenaam van het Spaanse rijk. Hij beklom de troon van Spanje in 1504, terwijl hij de soevereiniteit over de Nederlanden, die hij sedert 1494 persoonlijk uitoefende, behield.

Jammer genoeg overleed hij twee jaar later. Zijn zoon, Karel de Vijfde of Keizer Karel (1500-1558), die te Gent geboren was, werd in 1515 vorst der Nederlanden, in 1517 koning van Spanje en in 1519 keizer van Duitsland, terwijl hij, door de Pragmatieke Sanctie van 1549, de stichter van de XVII Provinciën of het 'Gewest Bourgondië' werd, waarvan Karel een 'onscheidbaar en ondeelbaar blok' wenste te maken.

Tijdens de regering van Keizer Karel deed de Renaissance haar triomfantelijke intocht in de Zuidelijke Nederlanden die, dank zij de eerste generatie van Belgische humanisten, tot een van de grootste intellectuele en wetenschappelijke centra van het Westen uitgroeiden. Tijdens zijn regering ontwikkelde zich in onze gewesten de Hervorming, die zo noodlottig zou worden voor de eenheid van het 'Gewest Bourgondië'.

Karel V beschouwde zichzelf steeds als Prins der Nederlanden, alhoewel hij koning van Spanje en keizer van Duitsland was, maar zijn zoon Filips II (1527-1589) gedroeg zich daarentegen enkel als buitenlands vorst, die zijn Belgische provinciën bestuurde vanuit het verre Spanje.

Hij vertrouwde de effectieve macht over zijn noordelijke provinciën toe aan landvoogdessen en gouverneurs, die de godsdiensttoorlog, welke de Nederlanden stoffelijk en zedelijk

(1467-1477) was less lucky; he came to a tragic end in the Battle of Nancy. The latter's daughter, Marie de Bourgogne, succeeded him in difficult circumstances. During her short reign, however, she was effectively supported by her husband, Maximilian of Austria, of the House of Hapsburg. The latter became Regent of the Duchy, on the early death of his wife, during the nonage of their son, Philippe le Beau (1478-1506).

As a consequence of the marriage between Marie de Bourgogne and Maximilian of Austria, our provinces passed under the authority of sovereigns, who reigned over territories far more important than our own. As a result, and for several centuries, the exercice of authority would consist of fluctuating local autonomies, within the framework of vast empires which were of primary concern to our Princes. Philippe le Beau—the son of Marie de Bourgogne and Maximilian—married Jeanne de Castille, known in history under the name of Jeanne the Mad. Through his wife, Philippe inherited the Spanish Empire. He became King of Spain in 1504, while retaining his personal lordship —since 1494—over the Netherlands.

Unfortunately, he died, two years later. His son, Charles Quint (1500-1558), born at Ghent, became Sovereign of the Netherlands in 1515; King of Spain in 1517; Emperor of Germany in 1519. By issuing the Pragmatic Sanction, in 1549, he created the 17 Provinces, or "Cercle de Bourgogne". He wanted to establish it as "an indivisible block, that cannot be shared". The present Belgian provinces formed the main part of the southern "Cercle" area.

Under Charles' reign, the Renaissance made its triumphal entry in the Southern Netherlands which, thanks to the first generation of Belgian humanists, became one of the main intellectual and scientific centres in the West. The same reign, however, saw the first stirrings of the Reformation movement, that would prove to be fatal to the "Cercle de Bourgogne".

Charles Quint always considered himself as Prince of the Netherlands, in spite of his crowns as King of Spain and Emperor of Germany. His son, Philip II (1527-1589) was a mere absentee sovereign, reigning over his Belgian provinces from his far-away Court of Spain.

He entrusted the actual power

länger eine feudale, sondern eine entscheidend nationale und zentralisierende Politik führte. Die Regierung dieses Fürsten dauerte lang und war gut. Sein Sohn Karl der Kühne hatte mit verschiedenen Schwierigkeiten zu kämpfen, die zum Schluss zu seinem tragischen Tod in der Schlacht bei Nancy (1477) führten. Maria von Burgund, seine Tochter, folgte ihm unter besonders schwierigen Umständen nach. Doch während ihrer kurzfristigen Regierung wurde sie durch ihren Gemahl, Maximilian von Habsburg, gestützt. Nach dem frühzeitigen Tod der Fürstin und während der Minderjährigkeit seines Sohnes Philipp des Schönen (1478-1506) übernahm Maximilian die Regentschaft über das Herzogtum.

Durch Heirat Marias von Burgund mit Maximilian von Österreich kamen unsere Provinzen unter die Macht von Fürsten, die über bedeutendere Gebiete herrschten. Während verschiedener Jahrhunderte war dann auch die Regierung unserer Länder beschränkt auf eine mehr oder weniger lokale Selbständigkeit, weil die Anzahl grosser Landesgebiete die Wachsamkeit unserer Fürsten fast völlig beanspruchte. Der Sohn Marias von Burgund, Philipp der Schöne, heiratete Johanna von Kastilien, in der Geschichte bekannt als Johanna die Wahnsinnige. Durch seine Frau wurde Philipp unerwartet Erbe des Spanischen Reiches. Er bestieg den spanischen Thron 1504, und behielt die Souveränität über die Niederlande, die er seit 1494 persönlich ausübte.

Leider starb er bereits zwei Jahre später. Sein Sohn Karl V. oder Kaiser Karl (1500-1558), der in Gent geboren ist, wurde 1515 Fürst der Niederlande, 1517 König von Spanien und 1519 deutscher Kaiser.

Durch die Pragmatische Sanktion von 1549 wird er der Gründer der 17 Provinzen, aus denen er ein unzertrennbares und unteilbares Ganzes zu machen wünschte. Die heutigen belgischen Provinzen bildeten den grössten Teil im Süden dieses Landes. Unter der Regierung von Kaiser Karl nahm die Renaissance ihren triumphalen Einzug in die südlichen Niederlande, die sich dank der ersten Generation belgischer Humanisten zu einem der grössten geistigen und wissenschaftlichen Zentren entfalteten.

Noch unter Kaiser Karls Regierung entwickelte sich die Reformation, die so verhängnisvoll für die Einheit des Burgundischen Reiches werden sollte.

Pays-Bas espagnols et d'autre part les Pays-Bas du Nord qui allaient connaître dès lors et jusqu'à nos jours, une destinée totalement différente de celle des provinces demeurées sous l'obédience de la couronne d'Espagne.

A la mort de Philippe II, les provinces belges devinrent cependant à peu près complètement indépendantes sous le règne de sa fille l'archiduchesse Isabelle (1556-1633) et de son beau-fils l'archiduc Albert (1559-1621). Sous leur règne fut signée la « Trève de douze Ans » (1609-1621), au cours de laquelle les Pays-Bas espagnols connurent une prospérité, hélas éphémère.

En l'année 1648, la « Paix de Munster » mit fin à la « Guerre de Quatre-Vingt Ans », mais elle consacra également la division du « Cercle de Bourgogne ». L'Escaut fut fermé à cette occasion et ce fut la ruine du port d'Anvers. Le règne de Louis XIV (1643-1715) devait amener pour les provinces belges une nouvelle suite de guerres et la perte d'importants territoires.

La « Paix d'Utrecht » (1713) mit fin à la « Guerre de Succession d'Espagne »; parmi ses clauses figurait la cession des Pays-Bas espagnols aux Habsbourg d'Autriche et ce fut pour les provinces belges le début d'une période nouvelle de leur histoire.

Cette période débuta sous des auspices peu favorables et Charles VI (1685-1740), le nouveau souverain des Pays-Bas méridionaux, dès lors appelés « Pays-Bas autrichiens », fut obligé de signer en l'année 1715 le très humiliant « Traité d'Anvers », dit « de la Barrière », qui fit des provinces belges une espèce d'état tampon.

Lors du décès de Charles VI, sa fille et héritière, l'impératrice Marie-Thérèse (1717-1780) se heurta aux ambitions territoriales de Louis XV, et ce fut à nouveau la guerre pour les provinces belges. Celle-ci se termina par la « Paix d'Aix-la-Chapelle » (1748). Entre-temps, en 1744, le duc Charles de Lorraine (1712-1780) était devenu gouverneur des Pays-Bas autrichiens. Sous son gouvernement, ceux-ci connurent une ère de réelle prospérité qui compte parmi les plus heureuses de l'« Ancien Régime ».
Sous le règne du fils de Marie-Thérèse, l'empereur Joseph II (1741-1790), le « Traité de la Barrière » fut aboli en 1781, mais les heurts entre l'absolutisme de ce « despote éclairé » et l'esprit particulariste des provinces belges allaient conduire celles-ci à un soulèvement populaire appelé la « Révolution braban-

ten onder bracht, niet konden beletten. Wanneer eindelijk de vrede hersteld was, bestond het 'Gewest Bourgondië' nog enkel in de herinnering : de Noordelijke Nederlanden waren gescheiden van de zuidelijke provinciën; en van toen af zouden de noordelijke een totaal andere lotsbestemming volgen dan de zuidelijke die onder het gezag van de Spaanse kroon waren gebleven.
Na de dood van Filips II werden de Belgische provinciën nochtans weer haast geheel onafhankelijk, onder de regering van zijn dochter aartshertogin Isabella (1556-1633) en van zijn schoonzoon aartshertog Albrecht (1559-1621). Tijdens hun voorspoedige regering werd het 'Twaalfjarig bestand' (1609-1621) gesloten. De Spaanse Nederlanden beleefden toen een helaas kortstondige welvaart.
In 1648 werd door de 'Vrede van Munster' een einde gemaakt aan de Tachtigjarige Oorlog, maar tegelijkertijd werd de verdeling van het 'Gewest Bourgondië' bekrachtigd. De Schelde werd gesloten, en dit betekende de dood van de haven van Antwerpen.
De regering van Lodewijk XIV van Frankrijk (1643-1715) bracht voor onze Belgische provinciën een nieuwe reeks oorlogen mee, en als gevolg daarvan, een aanzienlijk verlies aan grondgebied.
De 'Vrede van Utrecht' (1713) stelde een einde aan de Spaanse successie-oorlog. Een van zijn clausules bepaalde dat de Spaanse Nederlanden zouden worden afgestaan aan de Oostenrijkse Habsburgers.

Deze periode ving aan onder weinig gunstige voortekens, en de nieuwe vorst van de Zuidelijke Nederlanden die van toen af de Oostenrijkse Nederlanden werden genoemd, namelijk Karel VI (1685-1740), was verplicht in het jaar 1715 het zeer vernederende 'Verdrag van Antwerpen' of het zogenaamde 'Bareeltractaat' te ondertekenen, dat van de Belgische provinciën een soort van bufferstaat maakte.
Bij het afsterven van Karel VI was zijn dochter en erfgename keizerin Maria-Theresia (1717-1780) het slachtoffer van de landhonger van Lodewijk XV van Frankrijk. Weer werd oorlog gevoerd voor het bezit van de Belgische Provinciën. De oorlog werd besloten door de 'Vrede van Aken' (1748). Inmiddels was in 1744 hertog Karel van Lorreinen (1712-1780), gouverneur van de Oostenrijkse Nederlanden geworden.
Tijdens de regering van de zoon van Maria-Theresia, keizer Jozef II

over his Northern provinces to governesses or governors who were unable to prevent the material and moral disasters of religious wars in the Netherlands. When peace was eventually restored, the "Cercle de Bourgogne" had vanished. Its place had been taken by the Spanish Netherlands on the one hand, and the Northern Netherlands on the other hand. The latter were to take, to this very day, an entirely different course from that pursued by the regions retained under the Spanish crown.

At Philip II's death, the Belgian provinces became almost independant under the reign of his daughter, Archduchess Isabelle (1556-1633) and his son-in law, Archduke Albert (1559-1621). They saw the signature of the Twelve Years' Truce (1609-1621), during which the Spanish Netherlands flourished for a short while.

In 1648, the Peace of Munster put an end to the Eighty Years' War, but it also set the seal on the division of the "Cercle de Bourgogne". It marked the blockade of the Scheldt, and this brought about the ruin of the port of Antwerp. Under Louis XIV's reign (1643-1715), the Belgian territories were involved in a new series of wars, and losses of territories.

The Peace of Utrecht (1713) put an end to the Spanish War of Succession; one of its clauses gave the Spanish Netherlands to the Hapsburgs of Austria, and this marked the beginning of a new epoch in the history of the Belgian provinces.

The period set in under unfavourable auspices: Charles VI (1685-1740), the new sovereign of the Southern Netherlands—now being called Austrian Netherlands—was forced to sign, in 1715, the very humiliating Treaty of Antwerp, also called "de la Barrière", by which the Belgian provinces became a sort of buffer-state.

At Charles VI's death, Empress Maria-Theresa, his daughter and heiress, came into conflict with the ambitions of Louis XIV. Again, war flared up over the Belgian provinces. It ended with the Peace of Aix-La-Chapelle (1748). Meanwhile, in 1744, the Duke Charles of Lorraine (1712-1780) had become governor of the Austrian Netherlands. Under his reign the country knew true prosperity; it was one of the happier periods under the "Ancien Régime".

Karl V. betrachtete sich selbst als Fürsten der Niederlande, obwohl er König von Spanien und deutscher Kaiser war; doch sein Sohn, Philipp II. (1527-1589) fühlte sich als ausländischer Fürst, der seine belgischen Provinzen vom fernen Spanien aus regierte. Er betraute Statthalter und Gouverneure mit der Ausübung der Macht über die nördlichen Provinzen. Diese waren jedoch nicht imstande die Religionskrieg, welcher die Niederlande materiell und moralisch zugrunde richtete, zu verhindern. Als der Friede endlich wieder hergestellt war, bestand das Burgundische Reich nur noch in der Erinnerung : die nördlichen Niederlande waren von den südlichen Provinzen abgetrennt. Von der Zeit an sollte der Norden einer ganz anderen Schiksalsbestimmung folgen als der Süden, der unter der Macht der spanischen Krone geblieben war. Nach dem Tode Philipp II. wurden die belgischen Provinzen jedoch beinahe ganz unabhängig unter der Regierung seiner Tochter Isabella (1556-1633) und seinem Schwiegersohn Erzherzog Albrecht (1559-1621). Unter ihrer erfolgreichen Regierung wurde der »Zwölfjährige Waffenstillstand« geschlossen. Die spanischen Niederlande erlebten damals eine – leider nur kurze – grosse Wohlfahrt.

Der Friede von Münster machte 1648 ein Ende mit dem Achtzigjährigen Krieg, aber dadurch wurde die Teilung des Burgundischen Reiches entgültig.

Die Schelde wurde gesperrt und das bedeutete den Tod für den Antwerpener Hafen. Die Regierung Ludwigs XIV. von Frankreich brachte neue Kriege über die belgischen Provinzen und als Folge, bedeutende Gebietsverluste. Mit dem Frieden von Utrecht (1713) wurden die Spanischen Erbfolgekriege beendet. Eine der Klauseln bestimmte, dass die spanischen Niederlande an die österreichischen Habsburger abgetreten wurden. So wurde eine neue Geschichtsperiode für die belgischen Provinzen eingeleitet.

Es waren ungünstige Vorzeichen, unter denen diese Periode begann. Karl VI. (1685-1740), der neue Fürst der südlichen Niederlande, von nun ab als die österreichischen Niederlande bezeichnet, musste im Jahre 1715 den sehr demütigenden Vertrag von Antwerpen, auch »Bareeltractaat« genannt, unterzeichnen, der aus den belgischen Provinzen eine Art Pufferstaat machte.

çonne » (1789-1790). En 1790, fut déclarée l'indépendance d'une « Confédération des États Belgiques Unis », mais le désaccord entre les promoteurs de la révolution mit vite fin à cet embryon d'État belge, et avant que l'année 1790 ne fût écoulée, les provinces révoltées se trouvèrent à nouveau entièrement soumises à l'autorité de Vienne.

Toutefois les guerres de la jeune Révolution française allaient bientôt mettre non seulement fin à la « Période autrichienne », mais aussi à toute l'armature morale et sociale de l'Ancien Régime; la réalisation de l'indépendance des provinces belges, dont la Révolution brabançonne avait constitué une velléité particulièrement significative, allait s'en trouver retardée de plus de quarante ans.

L'entrée des troupes françaises dans les Payx-Bas autrichiens se fit au lendemain de la bataille de Jemappes (1792). L'occupation du territoire ne fut que de courte durée, car la victoire autrichienne de Neerwinden (1793) refoula l'envahisseur au-delà des frontières. Une nouvelle victoire française à Fleurus (1794) ramena les troupes de la Révolution en territoire belge. En 1795, les anciens Pays-Bas autrichiens, auxquels on joignit les territoires de l'ancienne principauté de Liège, devinrent partie intégrante de la Première République; ils furent divisés en 9 départements, tandis que tous les anciens privilèges furent abolis au profit des libertés nouvelles.

Le peuple belge ne put s'accomoder des mesures révolutionnaires qui lui furent ainsi imposées et ce fut la sédition de la « Guerre des Paysans » (1798-1799) qui fut des plus sévèrement réprimée.

Le coup d'état du 18 Brumaire de l'an VIII (9 novembre 1799) amena quelque détente. Le Premier Consul Bonaparte parvint à s'allier les sympathies de ses sujets belges, notamment par le Concordat de l'année 1801.

Cette pacification, accompagnée d'une brève période de prospérité, fut cependant suivie d'une nouvelle période de tension qui ne prit fin qu'avec la chute de Napoléon, devenu entre-temps empereur des Français. Tout comme le gouvernement de Charles de Lorraine avait été économiquement prospère pour les provinces belges, le règne éphémère de Napoléon lui fut particulièrement bénéfique. C'est sous son impulsion, en effet, que la grande industrie prit son essor en Belgique. Liévin Bauwens introduisit alors à Gand les premières machines mécaniques à tisser.

(1741-1790) werd in 1781 het 'Bareeltractaat' afgeschaft, maar de wrijvingen tussen het absolutisme van deze 'verlichte despoot' en de zin voor particularisme van de Belgische provinciën zouden deze laatste brengen tot een volksopstand die in de geschiedenis bekend staat als de 'Brabantse omwenteling' (1789-1790). Wel werd in de loop van dat laatste jaar de onafhankelijkheid van de 'Verenigde Belgische Provinciën' uitgeroepen, maar ingevolge onenigheden onder de leiders van de revolutie kwam er spoedig een einde aan de onafhankelijke Belgische Staat, en nog vóór het einde van 1790 waren onze opstandige provinciën weer volledig onderworpen aan het gezag van Wenen.

De oorlogen van de jonge Franse Republiek zouden nochtans zeer spoedig een einde maken, niet alleen aan het Oostenrijks tijdvak, maar tevens ook aan de zedelijke en maatschappelijke structuur van het oude regime; de verwezenlijking van de onafhankelijkheid der Belgische provinciën, waarvan de Brabantse omwenteling een veelbetekenende voorbode was geweest, zou daardoor enkele jaren worden uitgesteld.

Na de slag bij Jemappes (1792) rukten de Franse troepen de Oostenrijkse Nederlanden binnen. Deze bezetting was echter van korte duur, want door de Oostenrijkse overwinning bij Neerwinden (1793) werd de overweldiger over zijn eigen landsgrenzen teruggeworpen. Een nieuwe Franse overwinning te Fleurus (1794) bracht de troepen van de revolutie opnieuw aan de macht op Belgisch grondgebied, en in 1795 werden de voormalige Oostenrijkse Nederlanden gewoonweg ingelijfd bij de Eerste Republiek; de Belgische provinciën werden verdeeld in 9 departementen, terwijl al de vroegere voorrechten afgeschaft en door de nieuwe vrijheden vervangen werden.

Het Belgische volk kon zich niet voegen naar de revolutionaire maatregelen die men het wilde opleggen, en dit gaf aanleiding tot de 'Boerenkrijg' (1798-1799) die met geweld werd onderdrukt.

De staatsgreep van de 18de Brumaire van het jaar VII (9 november 1797) bracht enige ontspanning. Eerste consul Bonaparte slaagde er in de sympathie van zijn Belgische onderdanen te winnen, door het Concordaat van het jaar 1801. Deze pacificatie, die gepaard ging met een kortstondige periode van welvaart, werd nochtans spoedig gevolgd door een nieuwe periode van spanningen, waaraan slechts een einde kwam met

Under the reign of Emperor Joseph II (1741-1790), Maria-Theresa's son, the "Traité de la Barrière" was abolished, in 1781. Clashes between the "enlightened despot" 's absolutism and the particularistic mentality in the Belgian provinces culminated in a popular uprising called "Révolution brabançonne" (1789-1790). In 1790, the independence was proclaimed of a "Confédération des Etats Belgiques Unis". Disagreements between the promotors of the revolution, however, quickly killed this embryo of a Belgian State. Before the end of the year 1790, the revolting provinces were brought back under the authority of Vienna.

The wars of the young French Revolution, however, soon were to mark the end, not only of the "Austrian period", but also of the whole moral and social structures of the "Ancien Régime": as a result, the setting-up of independent Belgian provinces, of which the Revolution in Brabant had been a significant prelude, would be postponed for more than forty years.

French troops entered the Austrian Netherlands after the battle at Jemappes (1792). The occupation was short-lived, for the Austrian victory at Neerwinden (1793) threw the invader back beyond the borders. A new French victory, at Fleurus (1794) brought the revolutionary soldiers back on Belgian soil. In 1795, the former Austrian Netherlands, together with the old Principality of Liège, became an integral part of the First Republic. They were divided in 9 "départements". All ancient privileges were abolished, and the new liberties were proclaimed.

The Belgians found it impossible to accept the revolutionary measures imposed by the French. This led to the seditious "Peasants' War" (1798-1799), which, in its turn, was very severely repressed.

The coup d'état of 18 Brumaire, an VIII (November 9, 1799) brought some detente. Bonaparte, as Premier Consul, succeeded in winning sympathy among the Belgians, i.a. because of the 1801 concordat.

The pacification, and a short period of prosperity were followed by new tensions which only came to an end with Napoleon's downfall (in the meanwhile, the latter had become Emperor of the French).

Charles de Lorraine's government had created prosperity in the Belgian provinces. The same was true,

Nach dem Tode Karls VI. wurde seine Tochter und Erbin Maria-Theresia (1717-1780) Opfer des Landhungers Ludwigs XV. von Frankreich. Wieder wurde um den Besitz der belgischen Provinzen Krieg geführt. Dieser Krieg endete 1748 mit dem Frieden von Aachen. Inzwischen war 1744 Karl von Lothringen (1712-1780) Gouverneur der österreichischen Niederlande geworden. Die Jahre unter seiner Regierung können zu den glücklichsten und wohlhabendsten des »alten Regime« gerechnet werden. Unter der Herrschaft von Maria-Theresias Sohn, Kaiser Joseph II. (1741-1790) wurde im Jahre 1781 der »Bareeltractaat« abgeschafft. Doch die Reibungen zwischen dem Absolutismus dieses »aufgeklärten« Despoten und dem Sinn der belgischen Provinzen für »Partikularisme« führte zu einem Volksaufstand, der in die Geschichte als die brabantische Revolution (1789-1790) eingegangen ist. Wohl wurde im Laufe dieses letzten Jahres die Unabhängigkeit der »Vereinigten belgischen Provinzen« ausgerufen; aber wegen der Uneinigkeit der Führer dieser Rebellion war es bald vorbei mit diesem unabhängigen belgischen Staat. Noch vor Ende des Jahres 1790 waren die aufständischen Provinzen wieder völlig der Macht in Wien unterworfen. Die Kriege der jungen französischen Republik sollten jedoch sehr bald nicht allein dem österreichischen Zeitalter, sondern auch der sozialen und gesellschaftlichen Struktur des alten Regimes ein Ende machen. Die Verwirklichung der Unabhängigkeit der belgischen Provinzen, wovon die brabantische Revolution ein bedeutungsvoller Vorbote gewesen war, wurde dadurch um einige Jahre verzögert.

Nach der Schlacht bei Jemappes (1792) rückten die französischen Truppen in die österreichischen Niederlande ein. Die Besetzung dauerte allerdings nicht lange, denn durch den österreichischen Sieg bei Neerwinden (1793) wurden die Eindringlinge über ihre eigenen Landesgrenzen zurückgeworfen. Ein neuer französischer Sieg bei Fleurus (1794) brachte die Revolutionstruppen wieder auf belgischem Gebiet an die Macht. 1795 wurden die früheren österreichischen Niederlande einfach der ersten Republik einverleibt. Die belgischen Provinzen wurden in neun Departemente verteilt, die früheren Vorrechte wurden abgeschafft und durch neue Privilegien ersetzt.

Das belgische Volk konnte sich den revolutionären Massnahmen,

Le blocus continental contribua d'autre part à la création de l'industrie sucrière à base de betteraves. Le port d'Anvers, enfin, connut une nouvelle ère de prospérité.

Par le « Protocole de Londres » ou « Acte des VIII Articles » (1814), les Puissances européennes décidèrent la création d'un Royaume des Pays-Bas qui comprendrait tout l'ensemble des anciennes XVII Provinces, plus l'ancienne principauté de Liège qui était demeurée indépendante jusqu'à la chute de l'Ancien Régime. Guillaume Iᵉʳ d'Orange (1772-1840) fut désigné comme roi de ce nouveau royaume, avec pour tâche d'assurer la complète union des provinces des anciens Pays-Bas et d'en faire un véritable « amalgame ».

Ce nouvel état fut officiellement reconnu par le « Congrès de Vienne » (1814-1815), mais dès la rédaction et le vote de la Constitution du royaume, les difficultés surgirent, car celui-ci se révéla aussitôt comme n'étant pas la monarchie constitutionnelle et parlementaire escomptée. Il y eut d'autre part le problème des cultes qui fut une des causes principales de la dislocation du royaume, dès l'année 1830.

Le règne de Guillaume Iᵉʳ sur les provinces belges n'en fut pas moins économiquement fort heureux. En homme d'affaires habile, le chef du jeune royaume encouragea le développement de l'industrie naissante. C'est lui qui présida à la fondation de la « Société Générale des Pays-Bas pour favoriser l'Industrie Nationale » qui devint par la suite la Société Générale de Belgique. Il améliora le réseau routier et fit achever le canal Gand-Terneuzen. Quant au trafic maritime, il connut un très grand essor au départ des ports d'Anvers, Ostende et Nieuport. Rappelons ici également que c'est en 1819 que la première usine à gaz du continent fut construite à Bruxelles, tandis que les Cockerills installèrent au Pays de Liège les premiers hauts-fourneaux à coke.

En dépit de tous ces signes de prospérité, les deux communautés belge et hollandaise qui formaient le Royaume des Pays-Bas ne purent s'accorder et en septembre 1830 éclata, à Bruxelles, une révolution qui allait conduire à l'indépendance de la Belgique. Dès le 25 septembre fut constitué un Gouvernement provisoire qui proclama, le 4 octobre, l'indépendance des provinces belges. Un Congrès national, élu le 3 novembre, fut chargé de l'élaboration d'une nouvelle constitution et de l'élection d'un nouveau chef d'État,

de val van Napoleon, die inmiddels keizer der Fransen was geworden.

Evenals het bestuur van Karel van Lorreinen voor de Belgische provinciën voorspoedig was geweest op economisch gebied, zo was ook de kortstondige regering van Napoleon bijzonder gunstig voor ons land. Het is inderdaad onder zijn impuls dat de grootindustrie in België een grote vlucht kon nemen. Lieven Bauwens bracht de eerste mechanische weefgetouwen naar Gent.

De continentale blokkade droeg anderzijds ruimschoots bij tot de oprichting van de bietsuikerfabrieken, terwijl de haven van Antwerpen een nieuwe periode van welvaart tegemoet ging.

In het 'Protocol van Londen' of de 'Acte der VIII Artikelen' (1814) besloten de Europese mogendheden tot de oprichting van een Koninkrijk der Nederlanden, dat de voormalige XVII Provinciën zou omvatten, samen met het vroegere prinsbisdom Luik, dat tot aan de val van het oude regime zijn onafhankelijkheid bewaard had. Willem I van Oranje (1772-1840) werd aangeduid als vorst van dit nieuwe koninkrijk, met de opdracht de volledige eenmaking van de provinciën van de vroegere Nederlanden te verwezenlijken.

Deze nieuwe staat werd officieel erkend door het Congres van Wenen (1814-1815), maar nauwelijks kwamen het opstellen en de goedkeuring van de grondwet van het Koninkrijk ter sprake of allerlei moeilijkheden ontstonden, want het nieuwe koninkrijk bleek niet de gedroomde grondwettelijke en parlementaire monarchie te zijn. Bovendien werd het probleem van de erediensten een van de voornaamste oorzaken van de ontbinding van het koninkrijk in 1830.

De regering van Willem I over de Belgische provinciën was nochtans gunstig op economisch gebied. Als handig zakenman moedigde het staatshoofd van het jonge koninkrijk de ontwikkeling van de ontluikende industrie aan. Aan hem is o.m. de oprichting te danken van de 'Algemene Nederlandse Maatschappij ter begunstiging der Volksvlijt', die later de 'Société Générale de Belgique' zou worden. Hij verbeterde het wegennet en deed het kanaal Gent-Terneuzen voltooien. De zeevaart nam een grote uitbreiding ten bate van de havens van Antwerpen, Oostende en Nieuwpoort. Terloops zij vermeld dat in 1819, te Brussel, de eerste gasfabriek van het Europese vasteland werd gebouwd, terwijl Cockerill in het land van Luik

to an even larger extent, for Napoleon's short reign. He favoured the development of large-scale industries in Belgium. In those days, Lieven Bauwens set up the first mechanical weaving-looms.

The continental blockade, on the other hand, favoured the development of a sugar-beat based sugar industry. The port of Antwerp, finally, entered a new era of prosperity.

By the "Protocol of London", also called "Acte des VIII Articles", the European powers set up a Kingdom of the Netherlands, that included the old XVII Provinces as a whole, and the old Principality of Liège, which had remained independent until the very end of the "Ancien Régime". William I of Orange (1772-1840) was appointed King of the new Kingdom, and was entrusted with the task of achieving full union among the provinces of the old Netherlands, by integrating them.

The new state received official recognition at the Vienna Congress (1814-1815). Difficulties arose during the drafting and voting of the Kingdom's Constitution, which was not to be the basis of the constitutional and parliamentary monarchy that had been expected. The religious issue, on the other hand, was one of the main factors in the Kingdom's dislocation, in the year 1830.

William I's reign, nevertheless, brought prosperity to the Belgian provinces. The young King had an acute sense of business, and he promoted the expansion of the young industries. He presided over the creation of the "Société Générale des Pays-Bas pour favoriser l'Industrie Nationale" which subsequently became the "Société Générale de Belgique". He improved the network of roads and had the canal Ghent-Terneuzen completed. Maritime traffic developed considerably, from the ports of Antwerp, Ostend and Nieuwpoort. We might also mention the fact that the first gas factory on the Continent was built in Brussels, in 1819.

Despite all these indications of prosperity, the Belgian and Dutch communities in the Kingdom of the Netherlands were unable to agree with each other. In September 1830, a revolution broke out in Brussels, that was to lead to Belgium's independence. On September 25, a provisional Government was set up. It proclaimed the independence of the Belgian pro-

die man ihm auferlegen wollte, nicht fügen. Das war der Anlass zum »Bauernaufstand« (1798-1799), der jedoch mit Gewalt unterdrückt wurde.

Der Staatsstreich des 18. Brumaire des Jahres VII (9. November 1797) brachte einige Entspannung. Durch das Konkordat des Jahres 1801 glückte es dem Konsul Bonaparte, die Sympathie seiner belgischen Untertanen zu gewinnen. Dieser Entspannung, die mit einer kurzen Zeit der Wohlfahrt zusammenmenging, folgte jedoch bald eine neue Periode voller Unruhe, die erst durch den Sturz Napoleons endete, der inzwischen Kaiser geworden war.

Wie das Regime Karls von Lothringen für die belgischen Provinzen auf wirtschaftlichem Gebiet erfolgreich war, war auch die kurze Regierung Napoleons für unser Land besonders günstig. Durch seinen Antrieb nahm die Grossindustrie einen mächtigen Aufschwung. Lieven Bauwens brachte die ersten mechanischen Webstühle nach Gent, die kontinentale Blockade trug in grossem Masse zur Errichtung von Rübenzuckerfabriken bei und der Antwerpener Hafen ging wieder einer Zeit grosser Betriebsamkeit und grossen Wohlstands entgegen.

Im «Protokoll von London» oder der »Akte der VIII Artikel« (1814) beschlossen die europäischen Mächte die Gründung eines Königreiches der Niederlande, welches die früheren XVII Provinzen und das Fürstbistum Lüttich (das bis zum Fall des alten Regimes seine Unabhängigkeit bewahrt hatte) umfassen sollte.

Wilhelm von Oranien (1772-1840) wurde zum Fürsten dieses neuen Königreiches bestimmt, mit dem Auftrag, die völlige Eingliederung der Provinzen der früheren Niederlande zu verwirklichen. Der neue Staat wurde offiziell durch den Wiener Kongress (1814-1815) anerkannt. Aber kaum kamen Entwurf und Billigung der Verfassung des Königreiches zur Sprache, so ergaben sich allerlei Schwierigkeiten: das neue Reich schien nicht die erträumte grundrechtliche und parlamentarische Monarchie zu sein. Die hauptsächliche Ursache der Auflösung des Königreiches 1830 war das Problem der Gottesdienste. Die Regierung Wilhelm I. über die belgischen Provinzen war dabei wirtschaftlich sehr günstig. Als tüchtiger Geschäftsmann förderte das Staatsoberhaupt die Entwicklung der aufblühenden Industrie. Ihm ist die Gründung der »Algemene Neder-

cependant que la régence fut confiée au baron Surlet de Chokier. Le 4 juin 1831, le prince Léopold de Saxe-Cobourg fut élu comme roi des Belges et le 21 juillet suivant, il prêta le serment constitutionnel à Bruxelles.

En l'espace d'à peine 142 ans, cinq rois ont su assurer à la Belgique indépendante une place exceptionnelle au sein de la communauté des nations.

Le roi Léopold Ier (1790-1865) se proposa pour première tâche d'asseoir définitivement la souveraineté du jeune royaume, sous le signe d'une union nationale, qu'il sut maintenir durant quelque dix ans.

Au cours des années 1840-1850, le royaume connut deux crises importantes. La première, d'ordre politique, conduisit à la naissance des partis catholique et libéral. La seconde, de nature économique, trouva d'une part son origine dans les entraves à la libre navigation sur l'Escaut et de l'autre, dans la perte des marchés extérieurs due à une politique protectionniste des pays voisins.

Cette crise atteignit son comble lorsqu'une maladie de la pomme de terre provoqua la famine dans le pays (1847).

Le roi Léopold Ier réussit en 1863 à racheter à la Hollande le droit de péage sur l'Escaut, et ce fut aussitôt l'essor prodigieux du port d'Anvers qui devint, en quelques années, un des premiers du monde. Rappelons d'autre part que c'est sous son règne éclairé que fut inaugurée, en 1835, la première ligne de chemin de fer du continent, allant de Bruxelles à Malines.

Sous le règne de son fils Léopold II (1835-1909), qui fut particulièrement prospère et qui plaça la Belgique parmi les principaux pays industriels du monde occidental, le pays connut cependant deux crises, l'une politique, l'autre sociale, que la grande sagesse du roi sut toutefois conjurer au mieux des intérêts de chacun. La crise politique trouva naissance dans une « guerre » scolaire; la crise sociale, elle, fut déterminée par les revendications d'un prolétariat devenu conscient de sa puissance et désireux de faire valoir ses droits dans la vie politique, sociale et économique du pays. L'année 1885 vit la fondation du Parti Ouvrier Belge, tandis que les ouvriers catholiques, de leur côté, s'inspirèrent de l'encyclique « Rerum Novarum » (1891), en fondant des ligues et des syndicats démocrates-chrétiens.

Cette prise de conscience du prolétariat conduisit à d'importantes réformes sociales de même qu'à

de eerste met cokes gestookte hoogovens installeerde.

Ondanks de wezenlijke voorspoed konden de Belgische en Hollandse gemeenschappen, die het Koninkrijk der Nederlanden vormden, het samen niet best vinden, en in september 1830 brak te Brussel een omwenteling uit, die tot de onafhankelijkheid van België zou leiden. Op 25 september werd een voorlopige regering opgericht, die op 4 oktober de onafhankelijkheid van de Belgische provinciën uitriep. Een op 3 november gekozen nationaal congres werd belast met het opstellen van een nieuwe grondwet en het kiezen van een nieuw staatshoofd, terwijl het regentschap werd opgedragen aan baron Surlet de Chokier. Op 4 juni 1831 werd prins Leopold van Saksen-Coburg tot Koning der Belgen gekozen, en op 21 juli legde hij te Brussel de grondwettelijke eed af.

Koning Leopold I (1790-1865) beschouwde het als zijn plicht de souvereiniteit van het jonge koninkrijk definitief te vestigen in het teken van een Nationale Unie, die de koning gedurende 10 jaar kon doen handhaven.

Van 1840 tot 1850 moest het koninkrijk twee zware crisissen doorworstelen. De eerste, van politieke aard, gaf aanleiding tot het ontstaan van de katholieke en de liberale partij. De tweede berustte op economische gronden, en werd veroorzaakt, enerzijds door de belemmering van de vrije scheepvaart op de Schelde, anderzijds door het verlies van de buitenlandse markten als gevolg van de door de nabuurlanden gevoerde protectionistische politiek.

Koning Leopold I slaagde er in 1863 in, de tolrechten op de Schelde van Nederland af te kopen, en dit was het vertrekpunt van de opbloei van de Antwerpse haven, die in enkele jaren tijds een van de eerste ter wereld werd. Onder zijn verlicht bestuur werd in 1835 tussen Brussel en Mechelen de eerste spoorweglijn op het vasteland ingehuldigd.

Onder de bijzonder voorspoedige regering van zijn zoon Leopold II (1865-1905), die België een plaats bezorgde onder de voornaamste nijverheidslanden van de westelijke wereld, had het land nochtans twee crises te doorworstelen, de ene van politieke en de andere van sociale aard, die de koning door zijn grote wijsheid tot eenieders voordeel vermocht te overbruggen. De politieke crisis werd veroorzaakt door een 'schooloorlog'; de sociale crisis was het gevolg van de eisen van het proletariaat, dat nu bewust was van

vinces on October 4. A national Congress, elected on November 3, was entrusted with the drafting of a new Constitution, and the election of a new Head of State. Meanwhile, the regency was exercised by Baron Surlet de Chokier. On June 4, 1831, prince Leopold of Saxe-Coburg was elected King of the Belgians and, on the following July 21, he took the constitutional oath in Brussels.

In a period of 135 years, five Kings have granted Belgium as an independent country an outstanding status among the commonwealth of nations.

King Leopold I (1790-1865) made it his first task to consolidate for good the sovereignty of the young Kingdom, under the motto of national union, which he succeeded to uphold for ten years.

In the years 1840-1850, the Kingdom passed through two serious crises. The first one was political in nature, and resulted in the creation of the catholic and liberal parties. The second one was of economic nature, and originated partly in the obstacles to free navigation on the Scheldt, and partly in the loss of foreign markets, due to protectionist policies in the neighbouring countries.

The crisis reached its peak in a famine, caused by a potato disease (1847).

In 1863, King Leopold I succeeded in buying back from Holland the toll rights on the Scheldt. This led to Antwerp harbour's spectacular expansion; in a matter of years, it became one of the largest in the world. Under his enlightened reign the first railroad on the Contient, between Brussels and Mechelen, was opened.

Under the reign of his son, Leopold II (1835-1909), the country was highly prosperous, becoming one of the most industrialized areas in the Western world. The Kingdom, however, had to weather two crises, one of political, the other of social character. The King, in his wisdom, succeeded in solving both, in the interests of all concerned. The political crisis found its origin in a "schools' war"; the social crisis, on the other hand, was caused by the demands of the poverty-stricken classes who had become aware of their power and wanted to assert their rights in the country's economic, political and social affairs.

In 1885 the "Parti Ouvrier Belge" was established. Catholic workers, on the other hand, found inspiration in the encyclica "Rerum Novarum"

landse Maatschappij ter begunstiging der Volksvlijt« (später »Société Génerale de Belgique«) zu danken. Er verbesserte das Strassennetz und liess den Kanal Gent-Terneuzen fertigstellen, er liess durch Cockerill die Schwerindustrie im Lütticherland einführen. Die Seefahrt erfuhr einen grossen Aufschwung, zum Vorteil der Häfen von Antwerpen, Oostende und Nieuwpoort. Vermelden wir eben noch, dass 1819 in Brüssel die erste Gasfabriek Europas gebaut wurde.

Trotz der wirklichen Wohlfahrt konnten die belgischen und holländischen Staaten sich nicht gut vertragen und im September 1830 brach ein Aufstand aus, der zur Unabhängigkeit Belgiens führen sollte. Am 25. September wurde eine vorläufige Regierung gebildet, die am 4. Oktober die Unabhängigkeit der belgischen Provinzen ausrief. Ein am 3. November gewählter Nationaler Kongress wurde mit der Erstellung einer neuen Verfassung und der Wahl eines Staatsoberhauptes beauftragt. Die Regentschaft wurde Baron Surlet de Chokier übertragen. Prinz Leopold von Sachsen-Coburg wurde am 4. Juni 1831 zum König der Belgier gewählt. Am 21. Juli legte er in Brüssel den Eid auf die Verfassung ab.

König Leopold I. (1790-1865) sah es als seine Pflicht an, die Souveränität des jungen Königreiches im Zeichen der Nationalen Union, die er zehn Jahre lang behaupten konnte, zu festigen. 1840-1850 überstand das Reich zwei schwere Krisen. Die erste, von politischer Art, war Anlass zum Entstehen der Katholischen und der Liberalen Partei. Die zweite hatte wirtschaftliche Gründe und wurde verursacht einerseits durch die Sperrung der freien Schiffahrt auf der Schelde, andererseits durch den Verlust der ausländischen Märkte als Folge der Schutzzollpolitik der Nachbarländer.

1863 gelang es König Leopold I., den Holländern die Zollrechte der Schelde abzukaufen, und das war der Beginn des Aufblühens des Antwerpener Hafens, der in einigen Jahren der bedeutendste der Welt wurde. Unter König Leopolds aufgeklärtem Regime wurde 1835 zwischen Brüssel und Mechelen die erste Eisenbahnlinie des Kontinents eingeweiht.

Unter der besonders erfolgreichen Regierung seines Sohnes Leopold II. (1815-1905), der Belgien einen Platz unter den wichtigsten Industrieländern der westlichen Welt verschaffte, hatte das Land doch noch

l'instauration du suffrage universel, tempéré toutefois par le vote plural; le suffrage universel pur et simple ne devait être accordé qu'en 1919. En outre Léopold II signa, en 1909 peu avant son décès, la loi instituant le service militaire obligatoire.

Le règne de Léopold II fut d'autre part marqué par une œuvre personnelle et grandiose du roi : la création de l'État Indépendant du Congo avec lui-même comme chef d'État, en attendant que cet immense territoire aux richesses naturelles innombrables devint, en 1908, la colonie du Congo belge, et en 1960, la République du Congo-Léopoldville, qui a adopté depuis le nom de Zaïre.

A la mort de Léopold II, le roi Albert Ier (1875-1934) succéda à son oncle; son règne fut hélas bientôt marqué par une des pages les plus douloureuses, mais aussi des plus glorieuses de l'histoire de Belgique : sa participation héroïque à la Première Guerre mondiale.

La guerre finie, la Belgique pansa ses blessures et reprit sa place dans le concert des nations européennes, se mettant résolument à la pointe du progrès social et de la modernisation de son potentiel économique.

Le règne d'Albert Ier, que l'histoire appelait, déjà de son vivant, le Roi Chevalier, fut tragiquement interrompu le 2 février 1934 par la mort accidentelle du souverain à Marche-les-Dames, et c'est son fils aîné qui lui succéda sous le nom de Léopold III (né en 1901). A peine après un an de règne, le jeune roi fut cruellement éprouvé par la mort accidentelle de son épouse, la reine Astrid. Son règne débuta également sous le signe de cette grande tension internationale dont la Seconde Guerre mondiale fut le tragique aboutissement. Au cours de ce nouveau conflit, l'armée belge commandée par le roi Léopold III, comme celle de 1914-1918 avait été placée sous le commandement direct d'Albert Ier, se comporta avec le plus grand héroïsme, mais fut obligée à la capitulation au bout d'une campagne de 18 jours.

Le roi Léopold III, ayant été fait prisonnier, fut détenu jusqu'en 1945, d'abord en Belgique et ensuite en Allemagne où il fut transféré avec sa famille. En raison de son absence, le prince Charles fut nommé Régent du Royaume. Il le demeura du 20 septembre 1944 au 20 juillet 1950. Le 16 juillet 1951, Léopold III abdiqua en faveur de son fils aîné Baudouin Ier (né en 1930).

Le règne du jeune souverain débuta sous les meilleurs auspices, car au lendemain de la guerre, l'économie belge s'était en effet révélée

zijn macht en zijn rechten wenste te doen gelden in het politieke, sociale en economische bestel van het land.

De ontvouwing van het proletariaat leidde tot belangrijke sociale hervormingen en tot de instelling van het algemeen stemrecht, dat echter gedeeltelijk getemperd werd door een stelsel van meervoudig kiesrecht, zodat tot 1919 moest gewacht worden om het algemeen en enkelvoudig stemrecht door te voeren. Bovendien ondertekende koning Leopold II in 1909 op zijn sterfbed de wet op de militaire dienstplicht.

De regering van Leopold II werd anderzijds gekenmerkt door een persoonlijke en grootscheepse verwezenlijking van de koning : de oprichting van de onafhankelijke Kongostaat, waarvan hij zelf het staatshoofd werd, in afwachting dat dit onmetelijke grondgebied met zijn ontelbare natuurlijke rijkdommen in 1908 een Belgische kolonie zou worden, en in 1960 zijn onafhankelijkheid zou bekomen. Een jaar geleden nam de jonge staat de naam Zaïre aan,

Na zijn dood werd Leopold II opgevolgd door zijn neef Albert I (1875-1934). Tijdens zijn regering werd helaas een van de meest pijnlijke, hoewel tevens ook een van de meest glorierijke bladzijden uit de Belgische geschiedenis geschreven : zijn heldhaftige deelneming aan de eerste wereldoorlog.

Wanneer alles achter de rug was, heelde België op korte tijd de door de oorlog geslagen verwondingen, veroverde het spoedig opnieuw zijn plaats in de rij der Europese landen en was het met beslistheid deelachtig aan de sociale vooruitgang en aan de modernisering van zijn economisch potentieel.

De regering van Albert I, die tijdens zijn leven reeds door de geschiedenis tot de Koning-Ridder werd bestempeld, werd op 11 februari 1934 op tragische wijze afgebroken door het noodlottige einde van de vorst te Marche-les-Dames. Zijn oudste zoon volgde hem op onder de naam van Leopold III (geboren in 1901). Nauwelijks één jaar na zijn troonsbeklimming werd de jonge koning wreed beproefd door de tragische dood van zijn echtgenote, de betreurde Koningin Astrid. Zijn regering begon midden in de grootste internationale spanning, die haar ontknoping vond in de tweede wereldoorlog. Tijdens dit nieuwe conflict gedroeg het Belgische leger, aangevoerd door koning Leopold III evenals het leger dat in 1914-18 onder het bevel had gestaan van

(1891) and set up christian-democratic confederacies and unions.

The emergence of the poor classes brought about important social reforms, and the establishment of universal suffrage, tempered, however, by a plural voting system. Downright universal suffrage was granted only in 1919. Just before his death, King Leopold II signed, in 1909, the law introducing conscription.

Leopold II's reign, on the other hand, was marked by a personal, imposing royal undertaking: the creation of the Independent Congo State, with the King as Head of State. In 1908, this immense territory, full of natural resources, became the colony of the Belgian Congo. In 1960, it reached independence status, and in 1972 it changed its name into Zaïre.

On Leopold II's death, his nephew, King Albert I (1875-1934) succeeded to the throne. His reign, unfortunately, was marked by one of the greatest tragedies that ever befell Belgium: its heroic participation in World War One.

When the war was over, the country slowly recovered and started again to play its role in Europe, by setting the pace in social progress and improving its industrial equipment.

King Albert's reign—the monarch was called, in his own days, "the Knight-King"—was abruptly brought to an end by the King's accidental death, on February 2, 1934, at Marche-les-Dames. His eldest son succeeded to the throne under the name of Leopold III (born 1901). After a mere year, the King suffered the loss, in an accident, of his wife, Queen Astrid. His reign also saw the first symptoms of the great international tension that led to the tragic outbreak of the Second World War. In this new conflict, the Belgian army, under King Leopold III's command —just as the 1914-1918 Belgian army had resorted under Albert I's direct command—fought heroically, but was compelled to capitulate after an 18 days campaign.

King Leopold III, as a prisoner of war, was detained until 1945, first in Belgium, and subsequently in Germany, with his family. Because of the King's absence, his brother Charles was appointed Regent of the Kingdom. He was in office from September 20, 1944, to July 20, 1950. On July 16, 1951, Leopold III abdicated, in favour of his eldest son, Baldwin I (born 1930).

The young King's reign started

eine politische und soziale Krisenperiode zu durchkämpfen, die der König mit grosser Geschicklichkeit und zu jedermanns Zufriedenheit überbrücken konnte. Die politische Krise wurde verursacht durch den »Schulkrieg«. Die soziale Krise war das Resultat der Forderungen des Proletariats, das sich nun seiner Macht bewusst geworden war und seine Rechte in der politischen, sozialen und wirtschaftlichen Ordnung des Landes geltend zu machen wünschte. Die Entwicklung des Proletariat führte zu wichtigen sozialen Reformen und zum allgemeinen Stimmrecht. Dieses jedoch wurde zum Teil eingeschränkt durch das System des mehrfachen Stimmrechts, so dass man noch bis 1919 warten musste, um das wirklich allgemeine und einheitliche Stimmrecht einzuführen.

Auf seinem Sterbebett unterzeichnete Leopold II. (1909) noch das Gesetz über die militärische Dienstpflicht. Besonders gekennzeichnet wurde die Regierung Leopolds II. durch dessen persönliche Verwirklichung, nämlich den unabhängigen Kongostaat, dessen Staatsoberhaupt er selbst wurde, bis das unermessliche Gebiet mit seinen natürlichen Reichtümern 1908 belgische Kolonie wurde. Der Kongo erhielt 1960 seine Unabhängigkeit zurück und heisst jetzt Zaïre.

Nach dem Tode Leopold II. folgte sein Neffe, Albert I. (1875-1934). Während dessen Regierung wurden leider die schmerzlichsten, aber auch rühmlichsten Seiten der belgischen Geschichte geschrieben : seine heldenhafte Teilnahme am 1. Weltkrieg. Die Kriegswunden Belgiens heilten in kurzer Zeit, es eroberte bald wieder seinen Platz in der Reihe der europäischen Länder. Mit Entschlossenheit nahm es am sozialen Fortschritt und an der Modernisierung seiner Wirtschaft teil.

König Albert I., der schon zu Lebzeiten als «König-Ritter» in die Geschichte einging, verunglückte tödlich am 11. Februar 1934 zu Marche - les - Dames. Sein ältester Sohn (geboren 1901) folgte ihm unter dem Namen Leopold III. Kaum ein Jahr nach seiner Thronsbesteigung wurde der junge König durch den tragischen Tod seiner Gemahlin, der vom ganzen Volk betrauerten König ing Astrid, heimgesucht. Seine Regierung begann während der grössten internationalen Spannungen, die mit dem zweiten Weltkrieg endeten. In diesem neuen Konflikt hielt sich die belgische Armee, angeführt durch König Leopold III. ebenso tapfer

d'une grande vitalité, et son dynamisme étonna à ce point le monde que l'on n'hésita pas à parler du « Miracle belge ». Ce miracle de persévérance du génie industrieux du peuple belge se poursuivit sous le règne du nouveau roi.

Un des grands événements du règne de Baudouin Ier fut son triomphal voyage au Congo belge dans le courant de l'année 1955. Ce voyage attira une fois de plus l'attention admirative du monde entier sur l'immense œuvre civilisatrice accomplie en moins de 75 ans par la Belgique au centre de l'Afrique noire, où elle était parvenue à créer un immense empire largement ouvert à la prospérité industrielle et commerciale ainsi qu'aux progrès sociaux dignes d'un pays avant tout féru des plus hautes valeurs morales. L'année 1960 vit l'accession du Congo belge à l'indépendance, non sans de tragiques remous dont cette terre africaine est encore loin de s'être remise.

ARTS, SCIENCES ET LETTRES

Dans tous les domaines de la vie intellectuelle, artistique et littéraire, la Belgique a toujours été une terre particulièrement privilégiée.

Si elle ne peut s'énorgueillir, comme certains autres pays, d'un art préhistorique fort riche, ses musées archéologiques n'en possèdent pas moins de nombreux objets des époques paléolithique et néolithique qui témoignent du goût artistique des premiers Belges sur le plan des arts appliqués. Il faut toutefois attendre l'époque de La Tène pour découvrir les premières œuvres de sculpture proprement dite, trouvées dans le sol belge, et encore n'est-on point tout à fait certain qu'elles soient autochtones.

De l'époque gallo-romaine, les œuvres d'art conservées dans les musées belges, surtout au Musée Archéologique d'Arlon, sont déjà infiniment plus nombreuses. Notons de très belles sculptures – elles aussi peut-être encore importées – et de non moins belles œuvres en céramique et en verre, de fabrication incontestablement locale.

Au lendemain des invasions barbares, et surtout depuis le règne de la dynastie carolingienne, les arts connurent un épanouissement qui a pu se maintenir jusqu'à nos jours.

Ce premier essor, qui est connu dans l'histoire de l'art sous l'épithète de « renaissance carolingienne », présente un caractère essentiellement religieux. En littéra-

---

Albert I, zich met de grootste heldhaftigheid.

Koning Leopold III, die krijgsgevangen was gemaakt, bleef tot 1945 gevangen en werd toen met zijn gezin naar Duitsland gevoerd. Tijdens zijn afwezigheid werd prins Karel benoemd tot regent van het koninkrijk en bleef dit van 20 september 1944 tot 20 juli 1950. Op 16 juli 1951 deed Leopold III afstand van de troon ten voordele van zijn oudste zoon Boudewijn I (geboren in 1930).

De regering van de jonge vorst begon onder de gunstigste voortekenen. Na de oorlog had de Belgische economie inderdaad al dadelijk blijk gegeven van een grote levenskracht, en haar dynamisme verbaasde zodanig de wereld, dat men niet aarzelde te spreken van het 'Belgische wonder'. Dit wonder van volharding van het scheppend genie van het Belgische volk zet zich verder door onder de regering van de nieuwe koning.

KUNST, WETENSCHAPPEN EN LETTEREN

Op alle gebieden van het intellectuele, artistieke en literaire leven is België steeds een bijzonder bevoorrecht land geweest.

Wellicht kan het zich niet, zoals andere landen, beroemen op het bezit van een rijk gestoffeerde voorhistorische kunst, maar zijn archeologische musea bewaren toch talrijke voorwerpen uit de paleolithische en neolithische perioden, die getuigenis afleggen van de kunstzin der eerste Belgen op het domein van de toegepaste kunsten. Toch moet gewacht worden tot het La Tènetijdperk om de eerste werkelijke beeldhouwwerken te ontdekken, die opgegraven zijn uit de Belgische bodem, alhoewel men er niet zeker van is dat zij werkelijk hier ter plaatse zijn voortgebracht.

De kunstwerken uit het Gallo-Romeinse tijdvak die in de Belgische musea worden bewaard, voornamelijk in het Archeologisch museum te Aarlen, zijn heel wat talrijker. Wij vermelden hier zeer mooi beeldhouwwerk – dat misschien ook wel is ingevoerd – en niet minder mooie voorwerpen van aardewerk en van glas, waarvan hier kan beweerd worden, dat zij ter plaatse zijn vervaardigd.

Na de invallen der barbaren, en voornamelijk sedert de regering van de Karolingische dynastie, ontvouwen de kunsten een ongemene bloei, die tot op onze dagen onverzwakt is gebleven.

---

under the best auspices, for the Belgian economy showed a great vitality immediately after the war, so much so that people, abroad, were talking of "the Belgian miracle". This miracle of perseverance and industry among the Belgians continued under the new monarch.

A memorable event in King Baldwin's reign was the sovereign's triumphal voyage through the Belgian Congo, in 1955. This visit, once again, focused the attention of the world on the magnitude of the task accomplished in 75 years by Belgium in the heart of dark Africa. A vast empire had been built there, that was accessible to industrial developments and trade flows, and that also benefited from progress in the social field, in the spirit of the moral values upheld in the mother-country. In 1960, the Belgian Congo became independent, and this caused several tragic upheavals, of which the African country has not yet recovered.

ARTS, SCIENCE AND LITERATURE

Belgium has always been a particularly privileged area in all fields of intellectual, artistic and literary endeavour.

It cannot claim—as certain other countries can—to possess a wealth of prehistoric art, but the collections in the archeological museums indicate that the Belgians of the paleolithic and neolithic eras were gifted as tool designers. The first sculptures found in Belgian soil date from the La Tène period: it is not absolutely certain that they were made on the spot.

The works of art of the Gallo-Roman period in Belgian museums —particularly at Arlon—are far more numerous. They include fine pieces of sculpture—possibly also imported—and beautiful ceramics and glass objects, of undisputed local manufacture.

After the invasions by the barbarians, and primarily since the Carlovingian dynasty, the arts have flourished without interruption to this very day.

The first blossoming, known in art history under the term "carlovingian Renaissance", is essentially religious in character. In literature, the main theme was hagiography, although secular history was not entirely neglected. The carlovingian scriptoria, on the other hand,

---

wie die Soldaten, die 1914/18 unter dem Befehl von König Albert gestanden hatten. Leopold III. geriet bis 1945 in Kriegsgefangenschaft und wurde dann mit seiner Familie nach Deutschland gebracht. Während seiner Abwesenheit wurde Prinz Karl zum Regenten ernannt und blieb dies von 20. September 1944 bis 20. Juli 1950.

Am 16. Juli 1950 gab Leopold III. seinen Thron ab zu Gunsten seines ältesten Sohnes Baudouin I. (geboren 1930).

Der junge Fürst konnte seine Regierung unter günstigen Vorzeichen beginnen. Nach dem Kriege hatte die belgische Wirtschaft sofort ihre grosse Lebenskraft bewiesen und ihre Dynamik erstaunte die Welt so sehr, dass man nicht zögerte, von einem »belgischen Wunder« zu sprechen. Dieses Wunder von andauerndem schöpferischem Genie des belgischen Volkes setzt sich unter der Regierung des neuen Königs fort.

KUNST, WISSENSCHAFT UND LITERATUR

Auf allen Gebieten des intellektuellen, künstlerischen und literarischen Lebens ist Belgiens stets ein bevorzugtes Land gewesen.

Man kann sich nicht wie in manchen anderen Ländern einer reichen prähistorischen Kunst rühmen, doch besitzen seine archäologischen Museen viele Objekte aus dem Paläolithikum und Neolithikum, die Zeugnis vom Kunstsinn der ersten Belgier auf dem Gebiete der angewandten Kunst ablegen. Die ersten wirklichen Plastiken, die aus belgischem Boden ausgegraben wurden, stammen aus dem La Thène-Zeitalter. Doch ist es nicht sicher, ob diese Gegenstände hier hergestellt wurden.

Die Kunstwerke aus der gallo-römischen Zeit in belgischen Museen (vor allem dem Archäologischen Museum zu Arlon) sind zahlreicher. Wir erwähnen hier sehr schöne Plastiken (vielleicht auch eingeführte) und ebenso schöne Gegenstände aus Ton und Glas, wahrscheinlich eigener Herkunft.

Nach dem Einfall der Barbaren und besonders seit der Regierung der Karolinger entwickelten sich die Künste zu einer ungewöhnlichen Höhe.

Der erste «Kunstausbruch» in der Kunstgeschichte bekannt als die »Karolingische Renaissance«, ist vor allem sakral ausgerichtet. So nahmen in der Literatur die Lebens-

ture, l'hagiographie fut le principal genre, bien que l'histoire profane, elle aussi, ne fût point négligée. Les scriptoria carolingiens produisirent d'autre part d'admirables manuscrits enluminés, tandis que les ivoiriers se distinguèrent surtout dans la ciselure de diptyques, de statuettes votives et de plats de reliure.

Quelques monuments préromans datent également de cette époque, dont l'actuelle église paroissiale Saint-Ursmar, à Lobbes-sur-Sambre.

Au lendemain des invasions normandes, l'architecture romane s'affirma, d'abord en des sanctuaires encore modestes, mais dès le xie siècle avec des églises infiniment plus importantes, comme l'église Saint-Vincent à Soignies, l'église Sainte-Gertrude à Nivelles et l'église Saint-Denis à Liège. Sous le règne de Notger, le premier prince-évêque de Liège, la grande cité mosane, fut un foyer de très grande vie intellectuelle et spirituelle, dont la renommée s'étendait au loin. L'école cathédrale en était le centre et comptait, dès les premières années du xie siècle, des philosophes et des théologiens de premier plan.

Les manuscrits enluminés sont de plus en plus beaux et de plus en plus riches, cependant que les écrivains des xe-xiiie siècles sont toujours requis par l'hagiographie et la chronique; mais d'aucuns s'adonnent également aux gloses théologiques, amorçant ainsi les premières spéculations philosophico-mystiques, dont la Belgique allait bientôt devenir la terre d'élection.

Au cours des xie et xiie siècles, l'art belge – surtout mosan – s'illustra d'une manière exceptionnelle dans l'orfèvrerie, avec des artistes de la qualité d'un Renier de Huy, d'un Godefroid de Huy, d'un Hugo d'Oignies et d'un Nicolas de Verdun. Parmi leurs chefs-d'œuvre, citons les fonts baptismaux de l'église Saint-Barthélemy à Liège, de même que de nombreuses châsses.

La sculpture proprement dite, de même que la musique prirent alors également leur essor.

La fin du xiie siècle vit l'apogée de l'art roman belge, d'une part avec le château des Comtes à Gand, d'autre part avec la cathédrale de Tournai, aux cinq clochers imposants, dont le chœur, de construction plus tardive, relève cependant du plus pur gothique scaldien.

Ce fut ensuite l'efflorescence de l'art gothique avec des églises, des beffrois, des halles et des hôtels de ville, toujours plus somptueux les uns que les autres. Sur le plan profane, citons comme principales étapes : les halles d'Ypres, celles de

Deze eerste kunstontluiking, in de kunstgeschiedenis bekend als de 'Karolingische Renaissance', wordt bepaald door een essentieel godsdienstig karakter. Zo was in de letterkunde de hagiografie het meest beoefende genre, hoewel ook de profane geschiedenis niet werd veronachtzaamd. De scriptoria uit het Karolingische tijdvak hebben talrijke prachtige, verluchte handschriften nagelaten, terwijl de ivoorbewerkers zich vooral onderscheidden in het snijden van diptieken en van votiefbeeldjes.

Uit deze periode dagtekenen eveneens enkele pre-romaanse monumenten, waaronder de huidige parochiekerk van Sint-Ursmaar, te Lobbes-sur-Sambre.

Na de invallen van de Noormannen kwam de romaanse bouwkunst tot uiting, eerst in de vorm van betrekkelijk bescheiden heiligdommen, maar reeds in de 11de eeuw in omvangrijker kerken zoals de Sint-Vincentiuskerk te Zinnik, de Sint-Gertrudiskerk te Nijvel en de Sint-Dionisiuskerk te Luik. Onder het bestuur van Notger, de eerste prinsbisschop van Luik, werd deze grote stad aan de Maas een centrum van een zeer intens intellectueel en geestelijk leven, waarvan de faam zich tot ver over onze grenzen verspreidde.

De verluchte handschriften worden voortdurend rijker en mooier, terwijl de schrijvers van de 10de tot de 13de eeuw zich voornamelijk toelegden op het beschrijven van heiligenlevens en het schrijven van kronijken, waar anderen zich bezig hielden met de verklaring van godgeleerde teksten.

In de loop van de 11de en 12de eeuw werd de Belgische kunst – vooral in de Maasvallei – gekenmerkt door de uitzonderlijke bloei van de edelsmederij, met vermaarde kunstenaars zoals Renier van Hoei, Godfried van Hoei, Hugo d'Oignies en Nicolaas van Verdun. Onder hun meesterwerken verdienen vermeld te worden de doopvont in de Sint-Bartholomeuskerk te Luik, evenals talrijke reliekschrijnen.

De eigenlijke beeldhouwkunst en ook de muziek namen geleidelijk aan een hoge vlucht.

Het einde van de 12de eeuw was getuige van het hoogtepunt van de Belgische romaanse kunst, met het Gravenkasteel te Gent en de kathedraal van Doornik.

Toen kwam de bloei van de gotische kunst met kerken, belforten, hallen en stadhuizen, die hoe langer hoe weelderiger werden.

Op het gebied van de profane

produced admirable illuminated manuscripts; ivory carvers, in those days, also made diptychs, votive statuettes and binding plates.

The country still has a few pre-romanesque monuments, i.a. the present St. Ursmar parish church at Lobbes-sur-Sambre.

After the Norman invasions, romanesque architecture began to spread, first in modest sanctuaries but, from the 11th century onwards, in important churches such as St. Vincent at Soignies, St. Gertrude in Nivelles and St. Denis in Liège. Under Notger, first prince-bishop of Liège, the large city on the Meuse was a famous major centre of learning and devotion. The core of it was the cathedral school, where, from the early years of the 11th century onwards, high-ranking philosophers and theologians were teaching.

The illuminated manuscripts are increasingly more ornamented and rich. Writers, in the 10th-13th centuries, devote themselves to hagiography and the recording of chronicles. Some, however, also write theological commentaries, and the first philosophical-mystical meditations, which soon would loom very large in Belgium.

In the 11th and 12th centuries, Belgian art—particularly in the Meuse valley—excells in silver and goldware: famous names in this field include Renier de Huy, Godefroid de Huy, Hugo d'Oignies and Nicolas de Verdun. Among their masterpieces the baptismal font in St. Barthelemy church, Liège, and several reliquaries deserve to be mentioned.

The period also marks the beginnings of sculpture and music.

At the end of the 12th century, romanesque art in Belgium culminates, on the one hand in the Counts' Castle at Ghent, and on the other hand in the cathedral at Tournai, with its five imposing towers; the choir, of a later make, is in the unadulterated gothic style developed in the Scheldt valley.

Then came the full bloom of gothic, in churches, belfries, covered markets and city halls of increasing splendour. In secular building, the successive stages show the following landmarks: the covered markets at Ieperen, Brugge and Mechelen, the city halls in Brugge, Brussels, Leuven and Oudenaarde, the latter bringing us on the threshold of Flemish Renaissance. In

beschreibungen der Heiligen den grössten Platz ein, obwohl die säkulare Geschichte nicht vernachlässigt wurde. Die »Scriptoria« der Karolingischen Zeit haben viele prächtig illustrierte Handschriften hinterlassen und die Elfenbeinschnitzer wunderschöne Diptychon und Votivplastiken. Aus dieser Zeit stammen auch einige vorromanische Bauwerke, darunter die St. Ursmaarkirche in Lobbes-sur-Sambre.

Nach den Einfällen der Normannen breitete sich die romanische Baukunst aus, erst mit ziemlich bescheidenen Gotteshäusern, im 11. Jahrhundert bereits mit grösseren Kirchen, wie die St Vincentiuskirche zu Soignies, die St Gertrudiskirche zu Nivelles und die St Dionysiuskirche zu Lüttich. Unter der Verwaltung von Notger, dem ersten Fürstbischof von Lüttich, wurde diese grosse Stadt an der Maas ein Zentrum von sehr intensivem intellektuellem und geistigem Leben, dessen Ruhm sich bis weit über die Grenzen verbreitete.

Die bebilderten Handschriften wurden immer reicher und schöner. Im 10. bis 13. Jahrhundert wurden vor allem Heiligenleben und Chroniken geschrieben, auch Auslegungen von theologischen Texten. Die Goldschmiedekunst blühte im Laufe des 11. und 12. Jahrhunderts auf.

Im Maastal gab es weit und breit berühmte Silberschmiede wie Renier van Huy, Godfried van Huy, Hugo d'Oignies und Nicolas von Verdun. Zu ihren Meisterwerken gehören vor allem das Taufbecken in der St Bartholomäuskirche zu Lüttich sowie zahlreiche Reliquienschreine. Die eigentliche plastische Kunst und auch die Musik nahmen allmählich einen beträchtlichen Aufschwung.

Das Ende des 12. Jahrhunderts erbrachte als Höhepunkte der belgischen romanischen Kunst das Grafenschloss zu Gent und die Kathedrale zu Tournai.

Danach kam die Blütezeit der gotischen Kunst mit Kirchen, Belfrieden, Hallen und Rathäusern, die immer prachtvoller wurden. Wir denken hier an die Hallen von Ieper, Brügge und Mechelen, die Rathäuser von Brügge, Brüssel, Löwen und das von Oudenaarde, das bereits den Übergang zur flämischen Renaissance anzeigt. Von den kirchlichen Bauten muss man als Höhepunkte nennen die St Romboutskathedrale von Mechelen und die Frauenkirche in Antwerpen. Etwas

Bruges et de Malines, l'hôtel de ville de Bruges, ceux de Bruxelles et de Louvain et enfin celui d'Audenarde, dont la construction nous mène au seuil de la Renaissance flamande. Sur le plan religieux, il faudrait citer la plupart des églises belges d'avant le XVIe siècle, telles que la cathédrale Saint-Rombaut de Malines et l'église Notre-Dame d'Anvers, comme suprêmes aboutissements. Des églises moins imposantes sont Saint-Martin à Ypres; Notre-Dame de Pamele, à Audenarde; Notre-Dame, à Bruges; Notre-Dame, à Dinant; Notre-Dame de la Chapelle et la cathédrale des Saints-Michel et Gudule à Bruxelles; Sainte-Waudru, à Mons; Saint-Lambert et Saint-Paul, à Liège pour n'en citer que quelques-unes.

Dans le domaine des arts plastiques, il faut attendre la fin du XIVe siècle pour voir surgir des talents exceptionnels, en attendant le glorieux siècle des Van Eyck dont le sculpteur Claus Sluter fut le grand initiateur. C'est le miracle du réalisme « flamand » qui commence avec des artistes tant d'origine flamande que wallonne. Citons ici pêle-mêle, outre les frères Van Eyck: Roger van der Weyden, Hugo van der Goes, Thierry Bouts, Petrus Christus, Hans Memlinc et Gérard David.

Au même moment les polyphonistes « néerlandais » avec Guillaume Dufay, Gilles Binchois et Jean Ockeghem étonnent l'Europe, cependant que la tapisserie flamande commence également sa prodigieuse conquête du monde occidental.

Dès la fin du XIIIe siècle la littérature en langue vulgaire (en français et en flamand) fit son apparition dans les provinces belges. Le duc Jean Ier de Brabant, Hendrik van Veldeke, Jacob van Maerlant et Jean van Boendaele s'illustrèrent dans les lettres profanes flamandes, tandis que Hadewych, Béatrice de Nazareth et Ruusbroec l'Admirable donnèrent l'envol à la mystique.

La poésie courtoise et épique de langue française fleurit également dans les provinces belges. Citons ici Adenet le Roi et l'auteur anonyme d'« Aucassin et Nicolette », vraisemblablement originaire des environs de Thuin. A la cour des ducs de Bourgogne, vécurent les tout grands chroniqueurs que sont Amé de Montgesoie, Olivier de la Marche et Philippe de Commynes.

La théologie et la philosophie continuèrent toutefois à se servir de la langue latine qui demeura jusqu'à la fin de l'Ancien Régime, la langue universelle des sciences. Parmi les grands philosophes médiévaux d'origine belge, citons Siger de

bouwkunst moeten hier o.m. vermeld worden : de hallen van Ieper, Brugge en Mechelen, de stadhuizen van Brugge, Brussel, Leuven en tenslotte dat van Oudenaarde, waarmede wij reeds op de drempel staan van de Vlaamse renaissance. Op godsdienstig gebied moeten als hoogtepunten genoemd worden : de Sint-Romboutskathedraal van Mechelen en de Onze-Lieve-Vrouwkerk van Antwerpen. Minder indrukwekkende kerken zijn die van Sint-Martinus te Ieper, Onze-Lieve-Vrouw-van-Pamele te Oudenaarde, Onze-Lieve-Vrouw te Brugge, Onze-Lieve-Vrouw te Dinant, de Kapellekerk en de kerk van Sint-Michiel en Sinte-Goedele te Brussel, de kerk van Sint-Waltrudis te Bergen, van Sint-Lambertus en Sint-Paulus te Luik, om er maar enkele te noemen.

Wat betreft de plastische kunsten moeten we wachten tot het einde van de 14de eeuw, om enkele uitzonderlijke talenten te zien opdagen, in afwachting van de glorierijke eeuw der Vlaamse Primitieven, waarvan de beeldhouwer Claus Sluter de grote bezieler was. Het is het wonder van het Vlaamse realisme dat begint met kunstenaars van Vlaamse zowel als van Waalse oorsprong. Van Eyck, Rogier van der Weyden, Hugo van der Goes, Dirk Bouts, Petrus Christus, Hans Memling en Gerard David.

Op hetzelfde tijdstip wekken de Nederlandse polyfonisten met Guillaume Dufay, Gilles Binchois en Jan Ockeghem de bewondering van Europa, terwijl het Vlaamse tapijtwerk over heel de westelijke wereld verspreid wordt.

Van het einde van de 13de eeuw af verscheen de letterkunde in de volkstaal (in het Frans en in het Nederlands) in de Belgische provinciën. Hertog Jan I van Brabant, Hendrik van Veldeke, Jacob van Maerlant en Jan van Boendale, onderscheidden zich in de Vlaamse wereldlijke letterkunde, terwijl zuster Hadewijch en Jan van Ruusbroeck, de 'Wonderbare', als de grondleggers van de mystiek kunnen beschouwd worden.

De Franstalige hoofse en epische poëzie bloeide eveneens in de Belgische provinciën. Hier moeten wij melding maken van Adenet le Roi en van de anonieme schrijver van 'Aucassin et Nicolette', die waarschijnlijk afkomstig is uit de streek van Thuin. Aan het hof van de hertogen van Bourgondië leefden beroemde kroniekschrijvers : Amé de Montgesoie, Olivier de la Marche en Philippe de Commynes.

De godgeleerdheid en de wijsbegeerte bedienden zich echter van

the religious field, one should mention most of the Belgian churches prior to the 16th century, such as St. Rombaut cathedral in Mechelen, and Notre-Dame in Antwerp, as supreme achievements. Less imposing santuaries include St. Martin at Ieperen; Notre-Dame de Pamele at Oudenaarde; Notre-Dame at Brugge; Notre-Dame at Dinant; Notre-Dame de la Chapelle and St. Michael cathedral in Brussels; St. Waudru at Mons; St. Lambert and St. Paul in Liège,—to name but a few.

In the field of art, exceptional practitioners appear at the end of the 14th century; they announce the glorious century of the brothers Van Eyck, which was opened up by Claus Sluter, the sculptor. In that century, the miracle of "Flemish realism" unfolds, in the work of artists both of Flemish and Walloon origin. Besides Van Eyck, they include Roger van der Weyden, Hugo van der Goes, Thierry Bouts, Petrus Christus, Hans Memlinc and Gerard David.

Simultaneously, the "Dutch" polyphonists—Guillaume Dufay, Gilles Binchois and Jean Ockeghem—make Europe listen, and Flemish tapestry weaving also begins to conquer the Western world.

By the end of the 13th century, literature in the vernacular languages (French and Flemish) made its debut in the Belgian provinces. Jean I, Duke of Brabant, Hendrik van Veldeke, Jacob van Maerlant and Jan van Boendaele make their marks in secular Flemish writing, while Hadewych, Beatrijs van Nazareth and Ruusbroec-the-Admirable develop their mystical works.

Courtly and epic poetry in the French language is also being written in the Belgian provinces, i.a. by Adenet le Roi, and the anonymous author of "Aucassin et Nicolette", who probably came from the Thuin area. The great chroniclewriters Amé de Montgesoie, Olivier de la Marche and Philippe de Commynes belonged to the Court of the Dukes of Burgundy.

Theology and philosophy continued to be written in Latin, the universal language of science until the end of the "Ancien Régime". Great mediaeval philosophers of Belgian origin include Siger de Brabant, Henri de Gand, Gilbert de Tournai, David de Dinant and Godefroid de Fontaines.

The works by all these writers, poets, chroniclers, hagiographers,

weniger eindrucksvoll sind die Martinuskirche zu Ieper, die U.L. Frauvan-Pamele-Kirche zu Oudenaarde, die Frauenkirche zu Brügge, die Frauenkirche zu Dinant, die Kapellenkirche zu Brüssel, die St Waltrudiskirche zu Mons, St. Lambert und St Paulus zu Lüttich, um nur einige zu nennen.

Auf dem Gebiet der Plastik tauchen erst zu Ende des 14. Jahrhunderts einige ausserordentliche Talente auf. Mit Van Eyck und Claus Sluter setzte das Wunder des flämischen Realismus ein mit Künstlern von flämischen wie auch wallonischem Ursprung : Van Eyck, Rogier van der Weyden, Hugo van der Goes, Dirk Bouts, Petrus Christus, Hans Memling und Gerard David.

Zur zelben Zeit riefen die niederländischen Komponisten, u.a. Guillaume Dufay, Gilles Binchois und Jan Ockeghem in ganz Europa Bewunderung hervor. Auch die flämischen Wandteppiche waren berühmt und verbreitet in der ganzen westlichen Welt.

Ende des 13. Jahrhunderts gab es zum ersten Male nicht-wissenschaftliche Bücher in französischer oder niederländischer Sprache. Herzog Johan I. von Brabant, Hendrik van Veldeke, Jacob van Maerlant und Jan van Boendale treten in der weltlichen Literatur besonders hervor; Schwester Hadewijch und Jan van Ruusbroeck der »Wunderbare« gelten als die Begründer der Mystik.

Die französische höfische und epische Poesie blühte auch in unseren Provinzen. Hier müssen wir Adenet le Roi und den anonymen Dichter von »Aucassin et Nicolette« erwähnen, der wahrscheinlich aus der Gegend von Thuin stammte. Am Hofe der Herzöge von Burgund lebten berühmte Chronisten : Amé de Montgesoie, Olivier de la Marche und Philippe de Commynes. Theologen und Philosophen gebrauchten jedoch Latein, das bis zum Ende des alten Regimes die universelle wissenschaftliche Sprache blieb. Unter die grossen mittelalterlichen Philosophen belgischer Herkunft gehören Siger van Brabant, Hendrik van Gent, Gilbert van Tournai, David von Dinant und Godfried van Fontaines.

Die Werke dieser Dichter, Hagiographen, Chronisten, Philosophen und Mystiker wurden kopiert in reich mit Miniaturen geschmückten Manuskripten, die noch jetzt der Stolz der grossen öffentlichen Bibliotheken sind.

Brabant, Henri de Gand, Gilbert de Tournai, David de Dinant et Godefroid de Fontaines.

Les ouvrages de tous ces écrivains, poètes, chroniqueurs, hagiographes, philosophes et mystiques furent recopiés en des manuscrits pour la plupart richement enluminés qui font toujours l'orgueil des grandes bibliothèques publiques. Un des fonds les plus riches est certainement la Bibliothèque des ducs de Bourgogne, actuellement conservée à la Bibliothèque royale de Belgique (Bibliothèque Albert I er) à Bruxelles. A la fin du xve siècle, la Renaissance fit son apparition dans les provinces belges, non seulement en architecture, mais dans tous les domaines de la vie artistique et spirituelle. En peinture elle signifia plutôt une période de tâtonnement et de recherche dominée par le souci d'égaler les grands maîtres de la Renaissance italienne, bien que le xvie siècle donnât naissance à un des plus grands peintres spécifiquement flamands de tous les temps, Pierre Breughel l'Ancien. Citons parmi ses précurseurs ou ses contemporains de valeur, Joachim Patenier (un des premiers grands paysagistes), Quentin Metsys, Jean Gossart dit Mabuse, Bernard van Orley, Frans Floris, Lambert Lombard et Lancelot Blondeel, qui s'illustrèrent également dans d'autres arts, sans oublier Pierre Aertsen et J. Beuckelaer, de même que les portraitistes et les paysagistes de premier plan que compte ce siècle.

En architecture, citons la Maison du Greffe à Bruges, le palais de Marguerite d'Autriche à Malines, le palais des Princes-Évêques à Liège, ainsi que l'hôtel de ville et la Maison de la Hanse à Anvers. En sculpture, citons surtout Jean Mone, Jean Dubrœucq, Guyot de Beaugrant et Corneille de Vriendt. La tapisserie de Bruxelles et l'art du vitrail s'orientèrent alors également vers l'art renaissant avec des chefs-d'œuvre de la qualité la plus rare.

La vie intellectuelle suivit le même courant et l'humanisme s'imposa sur le plan européen avec Érasme, né à Rotterdam, mais qui vécut de nombreuses années à Louvain et à Bruxelles. A sa suite ce sont André Vésale, Dodonée, Jean le Maire de Belges, Mercator, Ortelius, Simon Stévin, Busbecq, Joost de Damhouder, Philippe Wieland, Juste Lipse et Marnix de Sainte-Aldegonde, qui fut surtout un grand écrivain politique.

En poésie, citons les disciples flamands de la Pléiade que sont Jean van der Noot et J.-B. Houwaert, ainsi qu'Anna Bijns, poétesse essentiellement catholique.

het Latijn, dat tot het einde van het oude regime de universele wetenschappelijke taal bleef. Onder de grote middeleeuwse filosofen van Belgische afkomst kunnen genoemd worden Siger van Brabant, Hendrik van Gent, Gilbert van Doornik, David van Dinant en Godfried van Fontaines.

De werken van al die schrijvers, dichters, kronijkschrijvers, hagiografen, filosofen en mystiekers werden gecopieerd in meestal rijk verluchte manuscripten, die nog steeds de trots van de grote openbare bibliotheken vormen.

Op het einde van de 15de eeuw ontlook de Renaissance in de Belgische provinciën, niet alleen in de kunst, maar op alle gebieden van het artistieke en spirituele leven. In de schilderkunst was zij vooral een periode van aarzeling en van zoeken, in het teken van het streven om de grote meesters van de Italiaanse Renaissance te evenaren, alhoewel in de 16de eeuw een van de grootste specifiek Vlaamse schilders van alle tijden, met name Pieter Breughel de Oude, leefde. Tot zijn voorlopers of zijn tijdgenoten die faam verwierven, behoren Joachim Patenier (een van de eerste grote landschapschilders), Quinten Metsys, Jan Gossaert ook genaamd Jan van Mabuse, Barend van Orley, Frans Floris, Lambert Lombard en Lanceloot Blondeel, die ook in andere kunsttakken roem verwierven, zonder Pieter Aertsen en Joachim Beuckelaer te vergeten, evenmin als de eersterangs portretten landschapschilders van deze eeuw.

Op het gebied van de bouwkunst verdienen vermelding : de griffie te Brugge, het paleis van Margaretha van Oostenrijk te Mechelen, het paleis der prinsbisschoppen te Luik, alsmede het stadhuis en het Hansegebouw te Antwerpen. Als beeldhouwers verwierven bekendheid : Guyot de Beaugrant en Cornelis De Vriendt. De Brusselse tapijtwevers en glazeniers volgden hetzelfde spoor, en produceerden meesterwerken van het zuiverste gehalte.

Het intellectuele leven liep daarmee parallel, het Vlaamse humanisme bekleedde in Europa een vooraanstaande plaats met Erasmus, die wel te Rotterdam was geboren, maar talrijke jaren doorbracht te Leuven en te Brussel. Verder moeten vermeld worden : Andreas Vesalius, Dodoneus, Jean le Maire des Belges, Mercator, Ortelius, Simon Stevin, Ogier Ghislain de Busbecq, Joost de Damhouder, Filips Wieland, Justus Lipsius en Marnix van Sint-

philosophers and mystics were transcribed in manuscripts, most of which are richly illuminated, and the proud possession of large public libraries. One of the richest collections is the Library of the Dukes of Burgundy, now in the Royal Library of Belgium (Albertina Library), in Brussels.

By the end of the 15th century, the Renaissance pervades architecture and all other sectors of artistic and intellectual activities in the Belgian provinces. In painting, this meant a period of groping and experimenting, with the aim of emulating the great masters of the Italian Renaissance. The 16th century, however, produced one of the greatest, specifically Flemish, masters of all times: Peter Breughel the Elder. Among his distinguished forerunners or contemporaries, we should mention Joachim Patenier (one of the very first landscape painters), Quentin Metsys, Jean Gossart called Mabuse, Bernard van Orley, Frans Floris, Lambert Lombard and Lancelot Blondeel, who all worked also in other media; further, Peter Hertsen and J. Beuckelaer, and many other remarkable landscape or portrait painters.

In architecture, the period saw the construction of the Record-Office in Brugge, Mary of Austria's Palace in Mechelen, the Palace of the Prince-Bishops in Liège, the city hall and the Hansa House in Antwerp. In sculpture, Jean Mone, Jean Dubroeucq, Guyot de Beaugrant and Corneille de Vriendt made their marks. Brussels tapestry and stained glass also underwent the inspiring influence of Renaissance aesthetics.

The ideas followed the same course: humanism prevailed in Europe with Erasmus, who was born in Rotterdam, but spent many years in Leuven and Brussels. In his wake, we discover Vesalius, Dodonaeus, Jean le Maitre de Belges, Mercator, Ortelius, Simon Stevin, Busbecq, Joost de Damhouder, Philippe Wieland, Justus Lipsius and Marnix van St. Aldegonde, —the latter being primarily a great political writer.

In poetry, the Flemish followers of the Pléiade included Jan van der Noot and J.B. Houwaert, and also Anna Bijns, who was, essentially, a Roman Catholic poet.

The 15th century Dutch polyphonists found proper continuators in such highly qualified artists as

Die Renaissance begann am Ende des 15. Jahrhunderts aufzublühen, nicht allein in der Kunst, sondern auf allen Gebieten des künstlerischen und geistigen Lebens.

In der Malerei war sie vor allem eine Periode von Zaudern und Suchen, im Bestreben die grossen Meister der italienischen Renaissance zu imitieren, obwohl im 16. Jahrhundert einer der grössten, typisch flämischen Maler aller Zeiten, Pieter Breughel der Ältere, lebte. Zu seinen Vorgängern gehören Joachim Patenier (einer der ersten grossen Landschaftsmaler), Quinten Metsijs Jan Gossaert (auch Jan van Mabuse genannt), Barend von Orley, Frans Floris, Lambert Lombard und Lanceloot Blondeel, die auch in anderen Kunstzweigen berühmt waren. Wir dürfen auch Pieter Aertsen und Joachim Beuckelaer nicht vergessen, auch nicht die sehr guten Porträt- und Landschaftsmaler dieses Jahrhunderts.

In der Architektur sind folgende Bauwerke erwähnenswert : die Griffie zu Brügge, der Palast von Margaretha von Österreich zu Mechelen, der Palast des Fürstbischof zu Lüttich, sowie das Rathaus und Hansegebäude in Antwerpen. Als Bildhauer traten hervor Guyot de Beaugrant und Cornelis De Vriendt. Auch die Brüsseler Wandteppichweber und Glasmaler stelten wertvolle Meisterwerke her. Das intellektuelle Leben lief mit den bildenden Künste parallel, der flämische Humanismus nahm einen führenden Platz in Europa ein mit Erasmus, der wohl aus Rotterdam stammte, aber zahlreiche Jahre in Löwen und Brüssel verbrachte. Ferner erwähnen wir noch folgende bekannte Namen dieser Epoche : Andreas Vesalius, Dodoneus, Jean le Maire des Belges, Mercator, Ortelius, Simon Stevin, Ogier Ghislain de Busbecq, Joost de Damhouder, Filips Wieland, Justus Lipsius und Marnix van Sint-Aldegonde, letzterer besonders geschätzt als politischer Autor.

Von den Dichtern sind die bekanntesten die flämischen Anhänger der »Pleiade«, Jan van der Noot, J.B. Houwaert und Anna Bijns, die vor allem als katholische Dichterin hervortrat.

Die niederländischen Komponisten des 15. Jahrhunderts fanden würdige Nachfolger in Philippus de Monte, Cypriaan de Rore, Roland de Lassus, Adriaan Willaert, Josquin des Prés, u.a.

Les polyphonistes néerlandais du XVe siècle trouvèrent de dignes continuateurs en des artistes de la qualité de Adrien Willaert, Josquin des Prés, Cyprien de Rore, Philippe de Monte, Roland de Lassus etc.

Dans le domaine des arts, la Contre-Réforme donna naissance au style baroque dont le plus illustre représentant – dans les provinces belges tout au moins – est incontestablement le grand Pierre-Paul Rubens. Citons aussi les noms d'Antoine van Dyck, de Jacques Jordaens, de Gaspard de Crayer, de François Snyders, d'Adrien Brouwer, de Jean Breughel de Velours, de Jean Fijt, de Jean Wildens, de David Teniers le Jeune et de Roland Savery.

Les grands sculpteurs baroques flamands et wallons sont Jean de Bologne qui fit carrière en Italie, les frères F. et J. Duquesnoy, Jean del Cour, Lucas Fayd'herbe ainsi que la dynastie des Quellins dont l'aîné est digne du génie de Rubens.

En ce qui concerne la musique et la littérature, le XVIIe siècle fut en Belgique un siècle de décadence, laquelle se prolongea jusqu'à l'aube du XIXe siècle. Notons toutefois que le plus grand poète classique hollandais Joost van den Vondel, est d'origine anversoise, tout comme le grand peintre Frans Hals, lui, est d'origine malinoise.

Dans le domaine des sciences, la Belgique continua à se distinguer avec Léonard Lessius, Jean et Mercure van Helmont, Jean Palfijn, Pierre Stockmans, F. Verbiest, Jean-Charles della Faille et bien d'autres, tandis que la vie religieuse fut dominée par un saint Jean Berchmans et un Jansénius, qui se trouve à l'origine du jansénisme français. Citons ici également le grandiose travail d'hagiographie fourni par Bolland dont l'œuvre se poursuit jusqu'à nos jours sous l'égide des « Bollandistes ».

Le XVIIIe siècle est intellectuellement et spirituellement bien pauvre. Citons néanmoins le prince Charles-Joseph de Ligne, qui fut une des personnalités littéraires les plus marquantes du XVIIIe siècle.

L'Académie impériale et royale des Sciences et Belles Lettres de Bruxelles fut fondée en 1769, sous le nom de « Société littéraire ». Sa bibliothèque qui comptait 40.000 volumes fut accessible au public dès 1785.

Parmi les savants belges de l'époque qui connurent quelque célébrité citons le baron de Poederlé, fondateur de la dendrologie, et le chimiste physicien et médecin, J.-B. van Mons.

Aldegonde, bekend als een politiek auteur van formaat. Onder de dichters zijn bekend : de Vlaamse discipelen van de Pleiade, met name Jan van der Noot, J.-B. Houwaert en Anna Bijns, een bij uitstek katholieke dichteres.

De Nederlandse polyfonisten van de 15de eeuw hebben waardige navolgers gevonden in kunstenaars van het gehalte van Cypriaan de Rore, Adriaan Willaert, Josquin des Prez, Philippus de Monte, Roland de Lassus e.a.

Op het gebied van de kunsten gaf de contra-reformatie aanleiding tot de barokstijl, waarvan de schitterendste vertegenwoordiger – in de Belgische provinciën althans – ontegensprekelijk de grote Pieter-Paul Rubens is. Naast hem moeten nog genoemd worden : Antoon van Dijck, Jakob Jordaens, Caspar de Crayer, Frans Snijders, Adriaan Brouwer, Jan Breughel, Jan Fyt, David Teniers de Jonge e.a.

De grote Vlaamse en Waalse beeldhouwers van het baroktijdperk zijn Jean de Bologne, die carrière maakte in Italië, de broeders F. en J. Duquesnoy, Jean del Cour, Lucas Fay-d'Herbe en het geslacht van de Quellins waaronder de oudste het genie van Rubens bijna bereikt.

Op het gebied van de muziek en de letterkunde is de 17de eeuw in België een tijdperk van verval dat duurde tot het begin van de 19de eeuw. We wijzen echter op de grote Nederlandse dichter Joost van den Vondel, die van Antwerpse afkomst was, evenals op Frans Hals die afkomstig was uit Mechelen.

België onderscheidt zich verder op het gebied van de wetenschappen met Leonard Lessius, Johannes en Mercurius van Helmont, Jan Palfijn, Pieter Stockmans, F. Verbiest, Jean Charles della Faille en talrijke anderen, terwijl het godsdienstige leven beheerst werd door Sint Jan Berchmans en Jansenius, de grondlegger van het Franse Jansenisme.

In de 18de eeuw was het met het intellectuele en geestelijke leven eerder armzalig gesteld. Men kan alleen wijzen op prins Charles-Joseph de Ligne, een vooraanstaande figuur uit de Europese letterkunde van die tijd.

De Keizerlijke en Koninklijke Academie voor Wetenschappen en Schone Letteren van Brussel werd in 1769 opgericht onder de oorspronkelijke naam van 'Letterkundige Maatschappij'.

Tot de Belgische geleerden van die tijd, die enige beroemdheid verwierven, behoren baron de Poederlé, de grondlegger van de boomkunde,

---

Philippe de Monte, Cyprien de Rore, Roland de Lassus, Adrien Willaert, Josquin des Prés, etc...

In the arts, the Counter-Reformation led to the development of baroque art, whose greatest exponent—at least in the Belgian provinces—undoubtedly is Peter-Paul Rubens. Others worth noting include A. van Dyck, Jacob Joraens, Gaspard de Crayer, Frans Snyders, Adriaan Brouwer, Jan Velvert Breughel, Jan Fijt, Jan Wildens, David Teniers the Younger and Roland Savery.

The great, Flemish and Walloon, baroque sculptors are Jean de Bologne who made his career in Italy, the brothers F. and J. Duquesnoy, Jean del Cour, Lucas Fayd'herbe and the Quellin line of descendants, the founder of which was as gifted as Rubens.

In music and literature, the 17th century is characterized by a decadence, that was to last until the eve of the 19th century. We should indicate, however, that the greatest Dutch classical poet, Joost van den Vondel, was of Antwerp stock, and that the great painter Frans Hals was born of Mechelen parents.

In the sciences Belgium produced such eminent personalities as Leonard Lessius, Jan and Mercurius van Helmont, Jan Palfijn, Peter Stockmans, F. Verbiest, Jean-Charles della Faille, and many more. Prominent in religion were St. John Berchmans, and Jansenius, who was the instigator of "jansénisme" in France. We also should mention the huge work, in hagiography, undertaken by Bolland, and continued, to this day, under the auspices of the "Bollandistes".

The 18th century is one of comparative intellectual and spiritual sterility. Outstanding, however, is Prince Charles-Joseph de Ligne, one of the century's greatest literary personalities.

The "Académie impériale et royale des Sciences et Belles Lettres" in Brussels was established in 1769, under the name "Société littéraire". Its library, of 40,000 books, was made accessible to the public in 1785.

Under the scientists who made a name in those days, there are baron de Poederlé, founder of

---

Die Gegenreformation war in der Kunst der Anlass zum Barockstil. Sein glanzvollster Vertreter – wenigstens in den belgischen Provinzen – war ohne Zweifel der grosse Peter Paul Rubens. Doch neben ihm müssen noch Anton van Dyck, Jakob Jordaens, Caspar de Crayer, Frans Snijders, Adriaan Brouwer, Jan Breughel u.a. genannt werden.

Die grossen flämischen und wallonischen Bildhauer des Barock sind Jean de Bologne, der in Italien Karriere machte, die Brüder F. und J. Duquesnoy, Jean del Cour, Lucas Fay-d'Herbe und die Familie der Quellins, von denen der älteste fast das Genie von Rubens erreichte.

Für Musik und Literatur war das 17. Jahrhundert eine Zeit des Verfalls, die bis zum Beginn des 19. Jahrhunderts dauerte. Wir weisen jedoch auf den grossen klassischen holländischen Dichter Joost van den Vondel hin, der aus Antwerpen stammte.

Belgien besass auch auf wissenschaftlichem Gebiet Gelehrte von Weltruf : Leonard Lessius, Johannes und Mercurius van Helmont, Jan Palfijn, Pieter Stockmans, F. Verbiest, Jean Charles della Failla und zahlreiche andere. Die Theologie und das kirchliche Leben wurden angeführt durch Sint Jan Berchmans und Jansenius, dem Begründer des französischen Jansenismus.

Im 18. Jahrhundert war es um das intellektuelle und geistige Leben ziemlich armselig bestellt.

Fürst Charles-Joseph de Ligne, eine ausserordentliche Figur in der europäischen Literatur dieser Zeit, ragt etwas einsam hervor.

1769 wurde die Kaiserliche und Königliche Akademie für Wissenschaften und Schöne Literatur von Brüssel unter dem Namen »Letterkundige Maatschappij« gegründet. Zu den belgischen Gelehrten dieser Zeit, die einige Berühmheit erwarben, gehören Baron de Poederlé, der Begründer der Baumkunde und der Chemiker, Biologe und Arzt J.B. van Mons.

Von den Malern erwähnen wir Pieter Verhaegen, den Genremaler J. Garemijn und die Klassizisten Cornelius Lens und Joseph Suvée, von den Bildhauern Laurent Delvaux, H. Fr. Verbruggen, Th. Verhaegen, O. de Marseille, Ch. van Poucke und G.L. Godecharle.

En peinture le post-rubénien Pierre Verhaegen voisine avec le peintre de genre J. Garemijn et les néo-classiques Corneille Lens et Joseph Suvée. Les sculpteurs sont Laurent Delvaux, H.-Fr. Verbruggen, Théodore Verhaegen, Olivier de Marseille, Charles van Poucke et G.-L. Godecharle, dont le style évolue de l'art baroque au néo-classicisme, en passant par les grâces du rococo.

La même évolution est à noter en architecture et on assiste entre autres à la reconstruction, en style encore baroque, des dernières maisons de la grand-place et à la construction, en style Louis XVI, de la place Royale et de la place des Martyrs à Bruxelles.

Les compositeurs André-Modeste Grétry et Fr.-J. Gossec, d'origine belge, firent à l'étranger une très brillante carrière musicale qui connut son apogée à Paris, cependant que l'incomparable Beethoven trouve ses racines à Malines, où son grand-père fut chantre à la cathédrale Saint-Rombaut.

Le début du XIXe siècle ne fut guère propice à l'épanouissement d'une vie artistique et intellectuelle fort intense. Notons cependant, au cours du premier quart de ce siècle, quelques hommes de lettres d'expression française, tels Ph. Lesbroussart et le baron de Stassart, cependant que le grand savant A.-J. Quételet, qui fut entre autres le fondateur de la statistique, commença alors sa brillante carrière. Cette époque vit également la construction de deux monuments néo-classiques particulièrement remarquables : le palais du prince d'Orange (l'actuel palais des Académies) à Bruxelles, et les locaux de la nouvelle université de Gand, qui venait d'être fondée par le roi Guillaume Ier. Parmi les peintres, citons les néo-classiques Odevaere et Paelinck, ainsi que l'Anversois Mathieu van Brée.

L'enthousiasme provoqué par l'indépendance de la Belgique, en 1830, eut immédiatement une très grande répercussion sur la vie artistique et intellectuelle belge.

En peinture ce fut aussitôt l'épanouissement d'une école romantique avec des œuvres grandiloquentes, mais point toujours d'excellente qualité. Leurs auteurs sont Gustave Wappers, Nicaise de Keyzer, Louis Gallait et l'extravagant Antoine Wiertz. Des artistes infiniment plus modestes et souvent plus talentueux sont le néo-classique F.-J. Navez, et les peintres de genre J.-B. Madou, et Fernand de Braeckeleer. Citons encore Alfred Stevens qui vécut surtout à Paris, ainsi que le beau

en de scheikundige, natuurkundige en geneesheer J.B. Van Mons.

Als schilders moeten genoemd worden : Pieter Verhaegen, een verre discipel van Rubens, de genreschilder J. Garemijn en de neoklassiekers Cornelis Lens en Joseph Suvée; als beeldhouwers : Laurent Delvaux, H. Fr. Verbruggen, Th. Verhaegen, O. de Marseille, Ch. Van Poucke en G.L. Godecharle.

Dezelfde evolutie voltrekt zich in de bouwkunst : heropbouw van enkele huizen zoals op de Grote Markt te Brussel en aanleg, in Lodewijk XVI-stijl van het Koningsplein en het Martelarenplein, eveneens te Brussel.

De toondichters André-Modeste Grétry en F.R. Gossec, beiden Belgen, maakten in het buitenland een schitterende carrière.

Het begin van de 19de eeuw was niet gunstig voor de ontplooiing van een intens artistiek en intellectueel leven. Toch zijn er in het eerste kwart van die eeuw enkele Franstalige letterkundigen te vermelden zoals Ph. Lesbroussart en baron de Stassart, terwijl de grote geleerde A.J. Quételet toen als schitterend wetenschapsmens debuteerde. Deze periode werd ook gekenmerkt door het bouwen van twee bijzonder merkwaardige neo-klassieke monumenten : het paleis van de Prins van Oranje (het huidige Academiënpaleis) te Brussel, en de lokalen van de nieuwe universiteit te Gent, die pas was opgericht door koning Willem I. Tot de schilders behoren de neo-klassiekers Odevaere en Paelinck, evenals te Antwerpen Mathijs van Brée.

De geestdrift, verwekt door de onafhankelijkheid van België in 1830, had meteen een zeer grote terugslag op het Belgische artistieke en intellectuele leven.

In de schilderkunst ontvouwde zich spoedig een bloeiende romantische school met hoogdravende, niet altijd verantwoorde werken; de schilders heten : Gustaaf Wappers, Nicasius de Keyser, Louis Gallait en de extravagante Antoon Wiertz. Meer bescheiden en meer begaafd zijn : de classicus J.F. Navez, de genre-schilders J.B. Madou en Ferdinand de Braeckeleer, verder Alfred Stevens, die vooral te Parijs verbleef, en de voortreffelijke historieschilder Hendrik Leys, wiens esthetiek en techniek hoofdzakelijk beïnvloed werden door de genre-schilders uit de Vlaamse en de Duitse Renaissance. Tot een latere generatie behoren de landschap- en dierenschilders Jozef Stevens, Jan Stobbaerts, Hippolyte Boulanger en Hendrik de Braekeleer. Het impres-

dendrology, and J.B. van Mons, chemist, physicist and physician.

In painting, there are Pierre Verhaegen, who worked in the manner of Rubens; the genre painter J. Garemijn; the neoclassical artists Corneille Lens, and Joseph Suvée. Sculptors worth mentionning are Laurent Delvaux, H. Fr. Verbruggen, Théodore Verhaegen, Olivier de Marseille, Charles van Poucke and G.L. Godecharle, whose work, after baroque beginnings and rococo developments, eventually showed neo-classical trends.

The same development is noticeable in architecture. The period registered the building, in Louis XVI style, of the "place Royale" and the "place des Martyrs", all in Brussels.

Belgian born composers André-Modeste Grétry ánd Fr. J. Gossec made brilliant careers in Paris. Beethoven's roots, on the other hand, are in Mechelen, where is grand-father was cantor at the cathedral.

The beginnings of the 19th century were not auspicious for the flourishing of artistic and intellectual activities. In its first quarter, there were a few writers in the French language, like Ph. Lesbroussart, and baron de Stassart. In those days also the great scientist A.J. Quételet, who is, i.a., the father of statistics, began his brilliant career.

During the period two remarkable monuments in neo-classical style were built: the Palace of the Prince of Orange (the present Palace of the Academies) in Brussels, and the housing facilities of the University in Ghent, newly founded by King William I. Painters, in those days, include Odevaere and Paelinck for neo-classicism, and Mathieu van Bree, from Antwerp.

The excitement generated by Belgium's independence in 1830 extended immediately to artistic and intellectual life in the country.

In painting it produced the flowering of a romantic school, producing theatrical canvases of rather dubious quality. Their authors were Gustave Wappers, Nicaise de Kayser, Louis Gallait, and the extravagant Antoine Wiertz. Among the more modest, but often also more gifted artists, one notes F.J. Navez, a neo-classical painter, and the genre painters J.B. Madou and

Eine ähnliche Entwicklung vollzog sich in der Baukunst. In dieser Zeit wurde der Märtyrerplatz und der Königsplatz, beide im Stil Ludwigs XVI., angelegt.

Die belgischen Komponisten André-Modeste Grétry und F.R. Gossec machten in Frankreich eine glänzende Karriere.

Der Beginn des 19. Jahrhunderts war der Entwicklung eines intensiven künstlerischen und intellektuellen Lebens nicht günstig. Doch sind im ersten Viertel dieses Jahrhunderts einige französischsprachige Schriftsteller zu erwähnen, wie Ph. Lesbroussart und Baron de Stassart. Der grosse Gelehrte A.J. Quetelet debütierte damals als glänzender Wissenschaftler. In dieser Zeit wurden auch zwei besonders bemerkenswerte klassizistische Bauwerke errichtet: der Palast der Prinzen von Oranien (heute der Sitz der Akademien) zu Brüssel und die neue Universität zu Gent, gegründet von König Wilhelm I. Zu den bemerkenswerten Malern dieser Zeit gehören die Neuklassiker Odevaere und Paelinck sowie der Antwerpener Mathijs van Brée. Die Begeisterung, über die Unabhängigkeit Belgiens 1830 sollte eine grosse Wirkung auf das künstlerische und geistige Leben haben.

In der Malerei entwickelte sich schnell eine blühende romantische Schule mit manchmal recht schwülstigen Werken. Maler dieser Zeit waren Gustaaf Wappers, Nicasius de Keyser, Louis Gallait und der extravagante Antoon Wiertz. Bescheidener und begabter sind J.F. Navez, der Genremaler J.B. Madou und Ferdinand de Braeckeleer, ausserdem Alfred Stevens, der jedoch meist in Paris lebte, und der vortreffliche Historienmaler Hendrik Leys, dessen Ästhetik und Technik hauptsächlich durch die Genremaler der flämischen und deutschen Renaissance beeinflusst war. Zu einer späteren Generation gehören der Landschafts- und Tiermaler Jozef Stevens, Jan Stobbaerts, Hippolyte Boulanger und Hendrik de Braeckeleer.

Der Impressionismus begann mit James Ensor, zu ihm gesellten sich später Willem Vogels, Hendrik Evenepoel und Rik Wouters. Die Malerei dieser Zeit hatte natürlich auch ihre realistischen und naturalistischen Meister und ihre nachimpressionistischen und symbolistischen Schulen, bevor die grossen Meister des flämischen Expressio-

peintre d'histoire Henri Leys, dont l'esthétique et la technique s'inspirèrent surtout des peintres de genre de la Renaissance flamande et allemande. D'une génération postérieure sont les paysagistes et animaliers Joseph Stevens, Jan Stobbaerts, Hippolyte Boulenger ainsi que Henri de Braeckeleer. L'impressionnisme débuta en Belgique avec James Ensor. Il compte dans ses rangs Guillaume Vogels, Henri Evenepoel, Émile Claus, Rik Wouters et Ferdinand Schirren.

La peinture belge d'alors connut également ses maîtres réalistes, naturalistes et plein-airistes. Parmi ces derniers, citons surtout Jean Degreef, Isidore Verheyden et Franz Courtens.

La Belgique eut encore ses écoles post-impressionniste et symboliste avant de nous révéler les grands maîtres de l'expressionnisme flamand dont les précurseurs, sont, outre James Ensor, Eugène Laermans, Jacob Smits et George Minne. Ces peintres expressionnistes sont Albert Servaes, Constant Permeke, Gust de Smet, Fritz van den Berghe, Jan Brusselmans et Edgard Tijtgat. Quant à l'école contemporaine, elle compte en son sein quelques maîtres surréalistes, des peintres « animistes », de même que toute une génération de peintres plus ou moins abstraits, encore en pleine évolution. Ces derniers eurent pour précurseurs, vers les années 1920, toute une école abstraite belge qui attend encore son heure de consécration sur le plan international.

La sculpture belge a suivi depuis 1830 une courbe à peu près parallèle à celle de la peinture. Il y eut tout d'abord les continuateurs de l'école néo-classique, avec Guillaume et Joseph Geefs et Eugène Simonis. D'aucuns les classent déjà parmi les romantiques, pour ne réserver l'épi-thète néo-classique qu'à Charles Fraikin. Il y eut ensuite des maîtres réellement romantiques comme Paul de Vigne, Charles van der Stappen, Jef Lambeaux et Julien Dillens; des maîtres plutôt impressionnistes comme Jules Lagae et Thomas Vinçotte; des sculpteurs d'allure symboliste comme George Minne, Égide Rombeaux, Victor Rousseau et Ernest Wijnants, tandis que Rik Wouters, peintre remarquable par ailleurs, peut être considéré comme un des plus authentiques représentants de la sculpture post-impressionniste.

Au lendemain de la première guerre mondiale, il y eut des sculpteurs expressionnistes et cubistes dont Oscar Jespers, Jozef Cantré et Henri Puvrez. Par la suite se révélèrent de jeunes artistes néo-classi-

sionisme debuteerde in België met James Ensor, en telt in zijn rangen Willem Vogels, Hendrik Evenepoel en Rik Wouters.

De Belgische schilderkunst van die tijd had natuurlijk ook haar realistische en naturalistische meesters en haar openluchtschilders.

België had zijn post-impressionistische en symbolistische scholen, alvorens de grote meesters van het Vlaamse expressionisme zouden opdagen, tot welks voorlopers James Ensor, Eugeen Laermans, Jakob Smits en George Minne behoren. Deze expressionisten zijn Albert Servaes, Constant Permeke, Gustaaf De Smet, Fritz Van den Berghe, Jan Brusselmans, Edgard Tijtgat. De hedendaagse school bezit enkele surrealistische meesters, 'animisten', evenals een hele generatie van abstracte schilders, die nog in volle evolutie zijn.

De Belgische beeldhouwkunst heeft sedert 1830 een vrijwel met die der schilderkunst gelijklopende evolutie doorgemaakt. Er waren in de eerste plaats de voortzetters van de neo-klassieke school met Willem en Jozef Geefs en Eugène Simonis. Soms worden ze tot de romantiekers gerekend, terwijl alleen Charles Fraikin als neo-classicus beschouwd wordt. Daarna kwamen de echte meesters van het romantisme, zoals Paul de Vigne, Charles Van der Stappen, Jef Lambeaux en Julien Dillens, de meesters die eer impressionisten kunnen genoemd worden, zoals Jules Lagae en Thomas Vinçotte, beeldhouwers met symbolistische strekking, zoals George Minne, Egidius Rombaux, Victor Rousseau en Ernest Wijnants, terwijl Rik Wouters, tegelijkertijd ook een merkwaardig schilder, kan beschouwd worden als een van de echtste vertegenwoordigers van de post-impressionistische beeldhouwkunst.

Na de eerste wereldoorlog traden de expressionistische en kubistische beeldhouwers onder wie Oscar Jespers, Jozef Cantré en Henri Puvrez op het voorplan. Later kwamen jonge neoklassieke kunstenaars aan de beurt, zoals George Grard en Charles Leplae, terwijl de allerjongsten onder de beeldhouwers de abstracte en non-figuratieve kunst huldigden.

Gedurende de tweede helft van de 19de eeuw behoren de Belgische architecten tot de eclectische stijl, terwijl de godsdienstige bouwkunst veeleer afgestemd is op de neo-byzantijnse, de neo-romaanse en de neo-gotische stijl.

De Vlaamse Renaissance bleef opgeld doen bij het bouwen van stad- en gemeentehuizen. De grootste

Ferdinand de Braekeleer. Other interesting artists are Alfred Stevens, who worked mainly in Paris, and Henri Leys, who specialised in historical evocations, and drew mainly from the technique and aesthetics of the Flemish and German Renaissance painters. A later generation produced the painters of landscapes and animals Joseph Stevens, Jan Stobbaerts, Hippolyte Boulenger, and Henri de Braeckeleer. Impressionism was launched in Belgium by James Ensor, and inspired Guillaume Vogels, Henri Evenepoel, Emile Claus, Rik Wouters and Ferdinand Schirren.

Flemish painting, in those years, also numbered realists, naturalists, and open-air artists. Noticeable, among the latter, were Jean Degreef, Isidore Verheyden and Franz Courtens.

As elsewhere in Europe, Belgium had its post-impressionist and symbolist schools, and moved on to expressionism, of which James Ensor, Eugène Laermans, Jacob Smits, and George Minne were the forerunners. The great expressionist masters were Albert Servaes, Constant Permeke, Gust de Smet, Fritz van den Berghe, Jan Brusselmans, and Edgard Tijtgat. The contemporary school consists of some surrealists, a number of "animists", and a whole generation of more or less abstract painters still in full development. The latter had, as forerunners in the twenties, a truly abstract Belgian school that is still awaiting international recognition.

Belgian sculpture since 1830 has followed an almost parallel curve to that of painting. First came the continuators of neo-classicism. Guillaume and Joseph Geefs, and Eugène Simonis, for some critics, already belong to the romantic epoch, and only Charles Fraikin is being viewed as a true neo-classical artist. Truly romantic masters were Paul de Vigne, Charles van der Stappen, Jef Lambeaux and Julien Dillens. Jules Lagae and Thomas Vinçotte worked in a more impressionistic vein. Symbolists included George Minne, Egide Rombeaux, Victor Rousseau and Ernest Wijnants. Rik Wouters, who also was a great painter, represents post-impressionist sculpture at its highest level.

After the first World war, cubist and expressionist sculptors, such as Oscar Jespers, Joseph Cantré, and Henri Puvrez, made their marks.

nismus erschienen. Zu den expressionistischen Vorläufern gehören James Ensor, Eugeen Laermans, Jakob Smits und George Minne. Die Expressionisten sind Albert Servaes, Constant Permeke, Gustaaf De Smet, Fritz Van den Berghe, Jan Brusselmans, Edgard Tijtgat.

Die heutige Schule besitzt einige surrealistische Meister, »Animisten«, ebenso eine ganze Generation abstrakter Maler, die noch in voller Entwicklung sind.

Die belgische Bildhauerei hat seit 1830 eine mit der Malerei beinahe parallellaufende Entwicklung erlebt. Zunächst waren da die Anhänger der klassizistischen Schule : Willem und Jozef Geefs und Eugène Simonis, die man manchmal zur Romantik rechnet, während nur Charles Fraikin als Neuklassiker gilt. Dann kamen die wahren Meister der Romantik : Paul de Vigne, Charles Van der Stappen, Jef Lambeaux und Julien Dillens, die Meister die eigentlich zu den Impressionisten gezählt werden können, so Jules Lagae und Thomas Vinçotte; Bildhauer mit symbolistischer Tendenz wie Georg Minne, Egidius Rombaux, Victor Rousseau und Ernest Wijnants; Rik Wouters, ein ebenso bemerkenswerter Maler, kann als einer der wahrsten Vertreter der nachimpressionistischen Bildhauerei betrachtet werden.

Nach dem 1. Weltkrieg traten die expressionistischen und kubistischen Bildhauer, vor allem Oscar Jespers, Jozef Cantré und Henri Pubrez hervor. Später kamen klassizistische Künstler an die Reihe mit George Grard und Charles Leplae, während die allerjüngsten unter den Bildhauern die abstrakte und unfigürliche Kunst vertreten.

In der zweiten Hälfte des 19. Jahrhunderts vertraten die belgischen Architekten den eklektischen Stil; die kirchliche Baukunst dagegen war mehr auf den neubyzantinischen, neu-romanischen und neu-gotischen Stil abgestimmt.

Die flämische Renaissance zeigte sich beim Bau von Rat- und Gemeindehäusern. Der grösste unter den belgischen Architekten dieser Epoche ist ohne Zweifel Jozef Poelaert, der Schöpfer des riesigen Justizpalastes von Brüssel. Neben ihm verdienen Erwähnung Lodewijk Roelandt, Alfons Ballat, Henry Beyaert, Jan-Jozef van Yserdijk, Jan de Bethune d'Ydewalle, Jan de Bethune d'Ydewalle, Jan de Bethune d'Ydewalle, Jan de Bethune d'Ydewalle und Joris Hellepatte. Ende des vorigen Jahrhunderts hatte auch der Jugend-

ques comme Georges Grard et Charles Leplae, alors que les tout jeunes sculpteurs viennent de découvrir, à leur tour, l'art abstrait et non-figuratif.

Durant toute la seconde moitié du XIXᵉ siècle, les architectes belges pratiquèrent le style éclectique, cependant que l'architecture religieuse s'orienta plutôt vers les styles néo-byzantin, néo-roman et néo-gothique.

Le style Renaissance flamande fut surtout proposé pour la conception des hôtels de ville et des maisons communales. Le plus grand des architectes belges d'alors est incontestablement Joseph Poelaert, l'auteur du gigantesque palais de justice de Bruxelles. Citons à ses côtés Louis Roelandt, Alphonse Ballat, Henry Beyaert, Maurice van Yzendijk, Jean de Béthune et Joris Helleputte.

Vers la fin du siècle dernier, le « modern style » trouva ses promoteurs belges en la personne de Paul Hankar, Victor Horta et Henry van de Velde. A une génération plus jeune appartiennent Huib Hoste, E. van Averbeke, Victor Bourgeois, J. Eggericx, Sta Jasinsky, G. Brunfaut et Leo Stijnen.

Les arts appliqués et industriels, de leur côté, connurent depuis l'avènement du « modern style », au début de ce siècle, un véritable renouveau.

Quant à l'art musical, il s'épanouit, au lendemain de la révolution de 1830, avec des maîtres de la classe d'Henry Vieuxtemps, César Franck, Guillaume Lekeu, Peter Benoit, Jan Blockx, Edgard Tinel, Auguste Gevaert, Paul Gilson, August de Boeck, Joseph et Léon Jongen. Parmi les maîtres modernes citons Auguste Bayens, Marcel Poot, Jean Absil et André Souris, sans oublier évidemment les tout jeunes maîtres de la musique atonale, sérielle et électronique.

Dans le monde des lettres, notons la plus belle émulation entre les littérateurs d'expression française et ceux de langue néerlandaise. Le tout grand nom de la période romantique est l'écrivain flamand Henri Conscience, auteur de romans populaires traduits dans toutes les langues; pour la période post-romantique un nom importe : celui de Charles de Coster, l'auteur de « Thyl Ulenspiegel ». Citons encore du côté français André van Hasselt et Octave Pirmez; du côté flamand Karel Ledeganck, Prudens van Duyse, Théodore van Rijswijck et Tony Bergmann, mais n'oublions point Guido Gezelle que d'aucuns considèrent comme le plus grand poète néerlandais après Vondel.

onder de Belgische bouwkundigen van die tijd is onbetwistbaar Jozef Poelaert, de schepper van het reusachtige Justitiepaleis van Brussel; naast hem verdienen een vermelding: Lodewijk Roelandt, Alfons Ballat, Henry Beyaert, Jan-Jozef van Yzendijk, Jan de Bethune d'Ydewalle en Joris Helleputte.

Omstreeks het einde van de vorige eeuw kreeg ook de 'moderne stijl' zijn Belgische volgelingen in de persoon van Paul Hankar, Victor Horta en Henry Van de Velde. Tot een jongere generatie behoren Huib Hoste, E. Van Averbeke, Victor Bourgeois, J. Eggerickx, Sta Jasinsky, G. Brunfaut en Leo Stijnen.

In de toegepaste en industriële kunsten kon sedert de doorbraak van de 'moderne stijl' in het begin van deze eeuw een verheugende herleving geconstateerd worden.

De muziek beleefde na de revolutie een grote opbloei met meesters als Henri Vieuxtemps, César Franck, Guillaume Lekeu, Peter Benoit, Jan Blockx, Edgar Tinel, August Gevaert, Paul Gilson, August de Boeck, Joseph en Léon Jongen. Tot de modernen behoren August Bayens, Marcel Poot en André Souris, terwijl de jongere generatie naar de beginselen van de atonale muziek en het twaalftonenstelsel componeert.

Tot de grote vituosen behoren Henri de Bériot, Eugène Ysaye, Arthur De Greef, Jef Denijn en Flor Peeters.

In de letterkunde bestaat een gezonde wedijver tussen de Franstalige en de Nederlandstalige auteurs. De grootste naam uit de romantische periode is die van de Vlaamse schrijver Hendrik Conscience, auteur van een groot aantal populaire romans die in meerdere talen werden vertaald; voor de post-romantische periode is een naam representatief : die van Charles de Coster, de schrijver van 'Thyl Ulenspiegel'. Onder de Franstalige schrijvers hebben André Van Hasselt en Octave Pirmez, onder de Nederlandsschrijvende Karel Ledeganck, Prudens Van Duyse, Theodoor van Rijswijck en Tony Bergmann werkelijke verdienste, terwijl Guido Gezelle algemeen beschouwd wordt als de grootste Nederlandse dichter na Vondel.

Omstreeks 1880 werd, in de Franstalige letterkundige kringen de groep van de 'Jeune Belgique' opgericht, waarvan Camille Lemonnier de voorloper was. Hij is met Georges Eekhoud en Eugène Demolder een van de voornaamste vertegenwoordigers van de Belgische naturalistische school. De Belgische 'Parnassiens' zijn de dichters Max Waller,

Subsequently, young neo-classical artists like Georges Grard and Charles Leplae were noted. The latest generation is trying to come to terms with abstract, non-figurative aesthetics.

During the whole 19th century, Belgian architects were given to eclecticism. In religions buildings, neo-byzantine, neo-romanesque, and neo-gothic trends prevailed.

Flemish Renaissance style was largely used for designing city and borough halls. The greatest Belgian architect, in those days, undoubtedly was Joseph Poelaert, the author of the huge Courts of Justice in Brussels. Other designers included Louis Roelandt, Alphonse Ballat, Henry Beyaert, Maurice van Yzendijk, Jean de Béthune and Joris Helleputte.

"Modern style", by the end of the century, had Paul Hankar, Victor Horta and Henry van de Velde as its promotors. A younger generation includes Huib Hoste, E. van Averbeke, Victor Bourgeois, J. Eggericx, Sta Jasinsky, G. Brunfaut and Leo Stijnen.

In the wake of the "modern style" movement, applied art and industrial design registered a breakthrough in the early years of this century.

Music, after 1830, registered such eminent composers as Henry Vieuxtemps, César Franck, Guillaume Lekeu, Peter Benoit, Jan Blockx, Edgard Tinel, Auguste Gevaert, Paul Gilson, August de Boeck, Joseph and Léon Jongen. Contemporary masters are Auguste Bayens, Marcel Poot, Jean Absil and André Souris. Young composers also are experimenting in atonal, serial and electronic music.

Literature saw challenging developments, both in French and Dutch. The great figure, in the romantic period, was the Flemish writer Henri Conscience, whose popular novels were widely translated. Another name commands attention in the post-romantic years: Charles de Coster, the author of "Thyl Ulenspiegel". André van Hasselt and Octave Permez also wrote in French. On the Flemish side, Karel Ledeganck, Prudens van Duyse, Theodore van Rijswijck, and Tony Bergmann kept the home fires burning, until Guido Gezelle appeared, the greatest poet in the Dutch language, according to some, since Vondel.

stil seine Anhänger in Paul Hankar, Victor Horta und Henry van de Velde. Zu der jüngeren Generation gehören Huib Hoste, E. Van Averbeke, Victòr Bourgeois, J. Eggerickx Sta Jasinsky, G. Brunfaut und Leo Stijnen.

In der angewandten und industriellen Kunst konnte seit dem Durchbruch des Jugendstils (Anfang dieses Jahrhunderts) eine erfreuliche Belebung beobachtet werden.

Die Musik erlebte nach der Revolution von 1830 ein grosses Aufblühen mit Meistern wie Henri Vieuxtemps, César Franck, Guillaume Lekeu, Peter Benoit, Jan Blockx, Edgar Tinel, August Gevaert, Paul Gilson, August de Boeck, Joseph und Léon Jongen. Zu den modernen gehören August Bayens, Marcel Poot und André Souris. Die jüngere Generation komponiert nach den Prinzipien der atonalen Musik und dem Zwölftonsystem.

Zu den grossen Virtuosen werden Henri de Bériot, Eugène Ysaye, Arthur De Greef, Jef Denijn und Flor Peeters gezählt.

In der Literatur herrscht ein gesunder Wetteifer zwischen französisch und niederländisch sprechenden Autoren.

Der grösste Name aus der romantischen Periode ist der des flämischen Schriftstellers Hendrik Conscience, der eine grosse Anzahl volkstümlicher Romane geschrieben hat, die in viele Sprachen übersetzt wurden.

Charles de Coster vertritt die Nachromantik, sein Roman »Tijl Ulenspiegel« gehört zur Weltliteratur. Unter den französischsprachigen Schriftstellern haben wir André Van Hasselt und Octave Pirmez. Zu den niederländisch schreibenden mit wirklichen Verdiensten gehören Karel Ledeganck, Prudens Van Duyse, Theodoor van Rijswijck en Tony Bergman. Guido Gezelle wird allgemein als der grösste niederländische Dichter seit Vondel anerkannt.

Um 1880 wurde in französisch sprechenden Literatenkreisen die Gruppe »Jeune Belgique« gegründet deren Vorläufer Camille Lemonnier war. Er ist mit Georges Eekhoud und Eugène Demolder einer der wichtigsten Vertreter der belgischen naturalistischen Schule. Die Dichter Max Waller, Albert Giraud und Iwan Gilkin gehören zum belgischen »Parnassus«; Impressionisten und

Vers 1880 débuta, du côté français, le renouveau de « La Jeune Belgique » dont Camille Lemonnier peut être considéré comme le précurseur. Il est avec Georges Eekhoud et Eugène Demolder, un des principaux représentants de l'école naturaliste belge. Les poètes parnassiens belges sont Max Waller, Albert Giraud et Iwan Gilkin; les impressionnistes et symbolistes sont Émile Verhaeren, Maurice Maeterlinck, Charles van Lerberghe et le romancier Georges Rodenbach.

La génération de l'entre-deux-guerres est surtout représentée par Franz Hellens, André Baillon et Charles Plisnier pour le roman; par Odillon-Jean Périer, Marcel Thiry et Henry Michaux pour la poésie; par Fernand Crommelynck et Michel de Ghelderode, pour le théâtre.

Les lettres flamandes virent apparaître leurs poètes et romanciers impressionnistes et symbolistes dans la revue « Van nu en straks », dont le premier numéro date de 1893. Parmi ses collaborateurs qui firent une brillante carrière, citons Prosper van Langendonck, August Vermeylen, Karel van de Woestijne, Stijn Streuvels et Herman Teirlinck.

A des générations plus jeunes, appartiennent les romanciers Félix Timmermans, Willem Elsschot et Gérard Walschap. Au lendemain de la première guerre mondiale, il y eut l'explosion de l'expressionnisme flamand avec les poètes Wies Moens, Marnix Gijsen (celui-ci se révéla depuis la seconde guerre mondiale comme un excellent romancier) et surtout Paul van Ostayen dont se réclament actuellement les jeunes poètes dits « expérimentaux ».

Esquissons enfin la vie des sciences belges depuis 1830, en rappelant que la vie universitaire dut être complètement réorganisée au lendemain de la révolution et qu'aux trois universités déjà existantes, vint s'en adjoindre une quatrième, celle de Bruxelles.

La plupart des savants belges furent attachés à ces établissements qui sont actuellement des foyers de vie scientifique particulièrement vivants.

Parmi les illustrations de la science belge nous ne citerons que quelques noms de réputation vraiment mondiale : l'historien Henri Pirenne ; le cardinal-philosophe Mercier, rénovateur de la philosophie thomiste; Zénobe Gramme, inventeur de la première dynamo industrielle; L. Baekeland, l'inventeur de la bakélite, ainsi que les médecins Jules Bordet et Corneel

Albert Giraud en Iwan Gilkin, de impressionisten en symbolisten zijn Émile Verhaeren, Maurice Maeterlinck, Charles van Lerberghe en de romanschrijver Georges Rodenbach.

De generatie tussen de twee oorlogen wordt vertegenwoordigd door Franz Hellens, André Baillon en Charles Plisnier voor de roman, door Odilon-Jean Périer, Marcel Thiry en Henry Michaux voor de poëzie, door Fernand Crommelynck en Michel de Ghelderode voor het toneel.

In de Vlaamse letteren schaarden de impressionistische en symbolistische dichters en romanschrijvers zich rond het tijdschrift 'Van nu en straks', waarvan het eerste nummer in 1893 verscheen. Tot zijn beste medewerkers rekenen we : Prosper Van Langendonck, August Vermeylen, Karel van de Woestijne, Stijn Streuvels en Herman Teirlinck.

Tot de jongere generaties behoren de romanschrijvers Felix Timmermans, Willem Elsschot en Gerard Walschap. Na de eerste wereldoorlog geschiedde de doorbraak van het Vlaamse expressionisme met dichters als Wies Moens, Marnix Gijsen (die zich sedert de tweede wereldoorlog heeft laten gelden als een uitstekend romanschrijver) en vooral Paul Van Ostayen, de voorloper van de 'experimentele dichters', waarvan Hugo Claus als de meest vooraanstaande beschouwd wordt.

De meer klassieke strekking wordt vertegenwoordigd door dichters als Raymond Herreman, Maurice Roelants en Richard Minne, eveneens door Urbain Van de Voorde, die echter eer essayist is dan wel dichter.

Willen wij een beeld schetsen van de evolutie der Belgische wetenschappen sedert 1830, dan moet eerst gezegd worden dat het universitaire leven na de omwenteling volkomen moest gereorganiseerd worden en dat aan de drie reeds bestaande universiteiten nog een vierde, die van Brussel, werd toegevoegd. De meeste van de Belgische geleerden zijn verbonden aan die inrichtingen, die thans bijzonder levenskrachtige centra van wetenschappelijk leven zijn.

We zullen hier slechts de namen vermelden van enkele geleerden met wereldfaam, als de geschiedschrijver Henri Pirenne; de kardinaal-filosoof Mercier, die de thomistische wijsbegeerte vernieuwde; Zénobe Gramme, die de eerste industriële dynamo vervaardigde; L. Baekeland, de uitvinder van het bakeliet; de twee Nobelprijswinnaars voor

In French writing a new trend, prepared by Camille Lemonnier, developed around 1880, with the "Jeune Belgique" movement, whose leaders, writing in a naturalistic vein, were Georges Eeckhoud and Eugène Demolder. Belgian "parnassiens" included Max Waller, Albert Giraud and Iwan Gilkin. Emile Verhaeren, Maurice Maeterlinck, Charles van Lerberghe and Georges Rodenbach, the novelist, represent impressionism and symbolism in literature.

In the generation between the two wars, Frans Hillens, André Baillon and Charles Plisnier are the main novelists; Odilon-Jean Périer, Marcel Thiry and Henry Michaux wrote poetry; Fernand Crommelynck and Michel de Ghelderode were the leading playwrights.

Developments in Flemish literature included the publication, in 1893, of the review "Van nu en straks", which was the forum for impressionist and symbolist poets and novelists, with contributions from such great writers as Prosper van Langendonck, August Vermeylen, Karel van de Woestijne, Stijn Streuvels and Herman Teirlinck.

Felix Timmermans, Willem Elsschot and Gerard Walschap belong to a later generation of novelists. After the first world war, the eruption was registered of Flemish expressionists, with the poetry by Wies Moens, Marnix Gijsen (who writes remarkable novels, since the second World war) and, above all Paul van Ostayen, now invoked by the young "experimental" poets as their leader.

Scientific developments in Belgium since 1830 were conditioned by a complete overhaul of university education after the revolution. A fourth university was added, in Brussels, to the already existing three establishments.

Most Belgian scientists have been closely connected with these seats learning and active research.

In the scientific sector, we will quote only a few, world-famous, names: Henri Pirenne, the historian; cardinal Mercier, the promotor of neo-Thomism; Zénobe Gramme, who built the first industrial dynamo; L. Baekelandt, who invented bakelite, and Jules Bordet and Corneel Heymans, the physicians who both were Nobel Prize laureates.

The great Belgian scientific orga-

Symbolisten sind Emile Verhaeren, Maurice Maeterlinck, Charles van Lerberghe und der Romancier Georges Rodenbach.

Die Gèneration zwischen den zwei Kriegen wird vertreten durch Franz Hellens, André Baillon und Charles Plisnier für den Roman, durch Odilon-Jean Périer, Marcel Thiry und Henry Michaux für die Poesie, durch Fernand Crommelynck und Michel de Ghelderode für das Theater.

In der flämischen Literatur gruppierten die impressionistischen und symbolistischen Dichter und Schriftsteller sich um die Zeitschrift »Van nu en straks«, deren erste Nummer 1893 erschien. Die wichtigsten Mitarbeiter waren Prosper Van Langendonck, August Vermeylen, Karel van de Woestijne, Stijn Streuvels und Herman Teirlinck.

Zu der jüngeren Generation gehören Felix Timmermans, Willem Elsschot und Gerard Walschap. Nach dem ersten Weltkrieg brachen die flämischen Expressionisten durch mit Dichter wie Wies Moens, Marnix Gijsen (der sich nach dem zweiten Kriege auch als ein ausgezeichneter Romanautor erwies) und vor allem Paul van Ostayen, dem Vorbote der »experimentellen« Dichter, von denen Hugo Claus als der wichtigste betrachtet wird.

Die mehr klassische Tendenz wird vertreten durch Dichter wie Raymond Herreman, Maurice Roelants und Richard Minne, auch durch Urbain Van de Voorde, der jedoch mehr Essayist als Dichter ist.

Um sich von der Entwicklung der Wissenschaften seit 1830 ein Bild zu machen, muss man wissen, dass das Hochschulleben nach der Revolution vollkommen neu organisiert werden musste. Den drei bestehenden Universitäten wurde noch eine vierte, die von Brüssel, hinzugefügt. Die meisten der belgischen Gelehrten arbeiten an den Universitäten, die jetzt besonders vitale Zentren wissenschaftlichen Lebens sind.

Wir nennen hier nur einige Namen von weltberühmten Gelehrten, den Historiker Henri Pirenne, Kardinal-Philosoph Mercier, der die thomistische Philosophie erneuerte, Zénobe Gramme, der den ersten industriellen Dynamo baute, L. Baekeland, der Erfinder des Bakelit, die zwei Nobelpreisträger für Medizin Jules Bordet und Corneel Heymans.

Es gibt in Belgien verschiedene

Heymans dont les noms figurent au palmarès des Prix Nobel de médecine.

Parmi les grands organismes scientifiques belges, citons la Fondation universitaire, le Fonds national de la Recherche scientifique, la Fondation Francqui, sans oublier les diverses académies dont la première en date remonte à la période autrichienne.

A l'exception de la Koninklijke Vlaamse Academie voor Taal- en Letterkunde, qui a son siège à Gand dans un hôtel de maître du XVIIIᵉ siècle, toutes ces académies ont leur siège au palais des Académies, à Bruxelles. La capitale belge est, en effet, depuis la fondation du royaume, en 1830, le grand centre intellectuel de la Belgique, celui où la vie de l'esprit est la plus intense et où se tiennent annuellement nombre d'expositions internationales, de même que d'innombrables congrès scientifiques. Ajoutons-y également que depuis quelques années, Bruxelles est le siège d'un des plus grands concours musicaux de réputation mondiale : le Concours reine Élisabeth.

Son palais des Beaux-Arts compte parmi les institutions les plus actives du genre, tandis que son Théâtre de la Monnaie est un des principaux théâtres lyriques du continent.

Rappelons enfin que Bruxelles est en passe de devenir la vraie capitale de l'Europe, depuis qu'elle est le siège de grands organismes européens tels que la Communauté économique européenne, l'Euratom etc. Cette capitale ne cesse de se métamorphoser depuis la fin de la IIᵉ Guerre mondiale pour mieux répondre à son destin européen, aussi de partout y surgissent des buildings de plus en plus hauts, tandis que ses artères ne cessent de se moderniser pour s'adapter à un trafic de plus en plus intense. Bruxelles, capitale de l'Europe, s'applique ainsi avec grandeur à ce rôle que lui envie plus d'une ville de l'ancien monde.

geneeskunde : Jules Bordet en Corneel Heymans.

Er bestaan in België verscheidene grote wetenschappelijke inrichtingen zoals de Universitaire Stichting, het Nationaal Fonds voor Wetenschappelijk Onderzoek, de Francqui-Stichting, en verschillende academiën, waarvan de oudste dagtekent uit het Oostenrijkse tijdvak.

Als Belgische hoofdstad is Brussel, sedert de oprichting van het koninkrijk in 1830, het grote intellectuele centrum van België, waar het geestesleven het drukst wordt beoefend, en waar jaarlijks tal van internationale tentoonstellingen en ontelbare wetenschappelijke congressen worden gehouden. Sedert enkele jaren is Brussel de zetel van een van de belangrijkste muziekwedstrijden met wereldfaam : de wedstrijd Koningin Elisabeth.

Het Brusselse Paleis voor Schone Kunsten is een van de meest actieve instellingen van die aard, terwijl de Muntschouwburg als een van de voornaamste schouwburgen van het vasteland geldt.

Laten we er verder aan herinneren dat Brussel ernstige kansen bezit om weldra de ware hoofdstad van Europa te worden. Van nu af aan hebben grote internationale instellingen er hun zetel en o.m. de Europese Economische Gemeenschap en het Euratom.

Sedert het einde van Wereldoorlog II ondergaat deze hoofdstad een bestendige gedaanteverwisseling om zich efficiënter te kunnen aanpassen aan de noden van een internationale hoofdstad. Overal worden hoge buildings gebouwd en de straten richten zich steeds naar een hoe langer hoe drukker wordend verkeer. Brussel, hoofdstad van Europa, legt zich aldus op grootscheepse wijze toe op deze uitzonderlijke hoedanigheid die haar door menige andere Europese hoofdstad benijd wordt.

nizations include the "Fondation universitaire", the "Fonds national de la Recherche scientifique", the Francqui foundation, and the various academies, one of which was created under the Austrian regime.

The "Koninklijke Vlaamse Academie voor Taal- en Letterkunde" has its seat in a patrician 18th century residence in Ghent. All the other academies are housed in the "Palais des Académies" in Brussels. The Belgian capital, since the establishment of the Kingdom in 1830, is the country's main intellectual centre where, every year, major international exhibitions and numerous scientific congresses are organised. In the last years, Brussels also is the location of one of the most prestigious musical events: the Queen Elisabeth competition.

Its "Palais des Beaux-Arts" is extremely active in various fields, and its "Théâtre de la Monnaie" is one of the leading opera houses on the continent.

Brussels is becoming Europe's capital, as the seat of the European Economic Community. The city is constantly undergoing transformations, in order to cope with its duties as a host to Europe: tall buildings are being erected, roads are being widened and improved for an ever increasing traffic. Brussels, as the capital of Europe, is trying to live up to the opportunity, which many a city in the Old World would be eager to take over.

grosse wissenschaftliche Institute, wie z.B. die Universitäre Stiftung, die Nationale Stiftung für wissenschaftliche Untersuchungen, die Francqui-Stiftung und verschiedene Akademien, von denen die älteste aus der österreichischen Zeit stammt

Die belgische Hauptstadt ist tatsächlich seit der Gründung des Reiches 1830 das grosse geistige Zentrum Belgiens. Hier ist das geistige Leben am intensivsten und jährlich werden hier unzählige Ausstellungen und Kongresse durchgeführt. Seit ein paar Jahren ist Brüssel Sitz eines der wichtigsten und weltberühmten musikalischen Wettbewerbe, des Königin-Elisabeth-Wettstreit.

Der Palais der Schönen Künste von Brüssel ist eine der aktivsten Institutionen dieser Art. Und die Nationale Oper (Opera de la Monnaie) gehört zu den besten Theatern Europas.

Erinnern wir noch daran, dass die Möglichkeit sehr gross ist, dass Brüssel die Hauptstadt Europas wird. Schon jetzt haben grosse internationale Organisationen ihren Sitz hier, so z.B. die Europäische Wirtschaftsgemeinschaft und das Euratom.

Seit dem Ende des zweiten Weltkrieges hat Brüssel ständig sein Gesicht verändert, um sich den Notwendigkeiten einer internationalen Hauptstadt zweckmässiger anzupassen.

Überall werden Hochhäuser gebaut und Strassen dem stets lebhafter werdenden Verkehr angepasst. Brüssel, die Hauptstadt Europas, bereitet sich auf grosszügige Weise auf diese besondere Aufgabe, um die sie von mancher anderen europäischen Hauptstadt beneidet wird, vor.

Table des matières - Inhoud - Contents - Inhalt